Called to be Mystics

EXPLORING OUR
SPIRITUAL JOURNEY

Called to be Mystics

EXPLORING OUR SPIRITUAL JOURNEY

ARLENE EINWALTER

SSSF

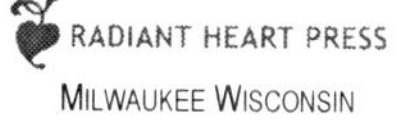
RADIANT HEART PRESS
MILWAUKEE WISCONSIN

Published by
Radiant Heart Press
an imprint of HenschelHAUS Publishing, Inc.
www.HenschelHAUSbooks.com

ISBN: 978159598-294-0
E-ISBN: 978159598-295-7
LCCN: 2013956600

Cover art by Janet Petersen, SSSF

Printed in the United States of America.

DEDICATED to Catholics and those of other faiths whose journey is taking them beyond Doctrine into an intimate union with the Divine.

TABLE OF CONTENTS

Acknowledgments

Robert Waterman, my teacher and spiritual companion whose teachings have inspired in me a deeper connection with God.

Melissa Pickett, whose encouragement and suggestions were invaluable as I worked to bring about this book.

Marla Juan-Darien, who critiqued the manuscript and offered many suggestions.

Francis Rothluebbler, a mentor over many years, who opened my eyes to new and wider vistas.

Sister Betty Tellesen, whose friendship and sharing led me to search for a more personal God.

My niece, Emy White, who first proofed this manuscript.

Sister Mary Carroll, Sister Theresa Engel, Sister Agnes Steiner, Sister Jane McKenzie, Alfreda Fielek, Rita Rubin, Victoria Frigo,

Naneki Elliott, and many more wonderful and encouraging friends.

Special thanks to: Allen Brizee of Loyola University, Maryland, for his patience in the final editing and helpful suggestions given as the book progressed.

Michael John Angeli, whose computer skills I could not have done without.

Reverend Thomas Sherbrook for his wonderful support and encouragement.

Rosemarie H. Berres for encouragement, support, and proofreading.

Kira Henschel, my publisher.

FOREWORD

am honored that Sister Arlene Einwalter considers me a mentor. While *Called to be Mystics* is her story, her experience of connecting and awakening to Soul and her transformational journey, it is also your journey and my journey. She will invite you into a grounded, common sense world and soon give you glimpses into a transcendence that enshrouds the ordinary. We all unfold our truth through life. Our lives are each a revelation to a way. So when, in her dedication, she says, this book is "DEDICATED to Catholics and those of other faiths whose journey is taking them beyond Doctrine into an intimate union with the Divine," she has already given us the key. As inspiring as doctrine is, it is a mental construct of God, whereas "an intimate union with the Divine" reveals truth as readily as breathing reveals life.

She begins: "One day, I looked up to the sky and said to God, "Teach me truth. Take me to the places I need to go and teach me the things I need to know so that I may find truth." Such a prayer is a covenant, perhaps even a primordial covenant now remembered. Prayer for me has become simply: the presence of complete love, while accepting the fulfillment of the heart's intention. We find the promise of our life by unlocking our hearts.

Following Sister Arlene's narrative, birth, or the intention to be born, begins a life journey. At birth, we face outward into the world and proceed taking on the shroud of our culture and family. Our guidance by parents and teachers is to find our vocation, our way to achieve and make a life. The focus is on success through vocation, family and community achievement. For the most part, we began this journey from a reality based on fear.

As we approach death, we reflect and extract meaning from our sojourn. For some, this is a disappointing process. On the other hand, if we haven't done so already, we let go of the fear-based accomplishments and realize that, all along, a deeper love was the true support and purpose of our journey. Our death becomes an anticipated initiation, a celebration of life in death. In dying, we awaken to a deeper sense of self.

For the mystic, reflection into meaning is there from the beginning. The mystic lives to awaken to a deeper sense of self, fulfilling this quest through the encounter of his own soul as the true self. Love is the basis of their reality. Death and rebirth is intrinsic to the journey. From the beginning, Sister Arlene sensed her life would be a mystic journey, translating her understanding of this into deeper meaning along the way.

The mystic path is challenging enough. Her path was in the context of the Catholic Church, an organization steeped in a tradition of great mystics, yet dominated by a tradition bound in administrative and doctrinal authority. In the simple narration of her life she illustrates the transformation that engenders within our character the ever increasing power of love, the primal authority of our soul, the inevitability of discovering that Jesus' message was to awaken to the Christ within.

In the mystic path, the way is not rebellion to authority. Authority is our friend and partner when we realize that the only source of self is from within and that within is within God. The only challenge to authority made by the mystic is that the mystic no longer accepts the definition of self that is projected by authority. Religious and laity join in a dance, an ascendance within the heart of God. When we are born again, we are all eligible to be priests. The mystic is born again into deeper and more profound levels in the "mansion of the Lord." Consider that there exists a primordial relationship to God within each of us, that guards and guides our way into realizing our place in the Christ.

Jesus placed in our hearts the most singular powerful message to ever be made explicit to humanity: "To love one another as I have loved you." Mystics knew this for millennium. To make this public to everyone was astounding. To consider that we have that capacity is revolutionary. How do we do this? "Seek first the kingdom of heaven and all else will be added to you." And, where is the kingdom. The "kingdom is within." These are the principle attributes of the Christ that He gave to us.

Sister Arlene provides a key with each chapter: *Beginnings, Intention, Identity, Harmony, Love, Worthiness, Presence, Creativity,* and *Healing.* Her life is one of service. In the reflexive relationship of server to service, the inner Christ is born as a transformational consequence of giving and receiving love. As such, it is a heroine's journey, a grail's quest. One strives outside to receive inside. She reminds us that our lives are a conversation between heaven and earth, of soul and relationship, in everything that we do. She reminds us that our identity is what we decide based on that conversation.

We discover that we are guided by an inner voice and the whispering of the saints, sages and angels who guide humanity, even ours. In the end, we must strive to be holy, because that's what we are. Holy, however, is an internal relationship rather than a standard, external image, fame, status, or power. Who knows what is holy? Well, holy does.

Jesus identified Himself as the Christ and often by the attributes of the Christ. He was the embodiment. Each of us is made in the same way, yet to different degrees of development and manifestation.

As a School Sister of Saint Francis, Sister Arlene, through ritual, received an anointing as the "bride of Christ." At the time this occurred, it was a mystery. Like all marriages the consummation is through union with the betrothed. The union reveals itself inwardly over time and gives birth to itself in our lives through service. In this way, she begins with the story of her life and how life is a process of unfolding and transformation as the whole person immerges from within. The consummate educator, she has designed each chapter with homework to assist the reader in exploring how the stories and principles become part of their everyday living. She gives us the practical tools, as mystics, to live the unfolding Christ.

I was surprised by Chapter Nine, *Healing.* The tone changed and it read like a manual on death and dying. Then I got it when she reviewed Kubler-Ross' phases of grief. I realized that phases of grief are the same as the phases of living. The character building process that challenge us in life are death and rebirth experiences. We have heard this admonition before: "to be born again." Ross' phases are: Denial, Bargaining, Anger, Depression, and Acceptance. Life will always be what it is, which is God's way of providing precisely what we need to respond to in order to remember, awaken, and to initiate a deeper and more conscious self.

Sister Arlene's motto for her grief work, "Grief is not a problem to be solved; rather it is a process whereby we can choose to integrate it into our lives, thereby becoming a healthier and holier person" is as readily a motto for her life. So, as you arrive at Chapter Nine, also substitute life each time you read death and see what insight arises for you. Perhaps each of us is the grieving person, longing to go home. So each time Sister Arlene shares a story of grief, put yourself in that person's place. The reflection resolves some aspect of life. The same mystery that greets us at death, greets us in the sequential rebirths of our life. This is the way of the mystic.

—Robert D. Waterman, Ed.D.

Dr. Waterman's life as a conscious student and teacher of spiritual understanding and realization began as a youth, looking up at the stars. He is founder and President Emeritus of Southwestern College, an accredited graduate school for counselors, using a spiritually based curriculum. He now teaches spiritual classes in the United States and Europe. In addition to the Mystery School, he practices and teaches Noetic Balancing, a consciousness approach to personal transformation.

He is author of *Footprints of Eternity: Ancient Wisdom Applied to Modern Psychology, Eyes Made of Soul: the Theory and Practice of Noetic Balancing*, and *The Mandala of the Soul: the Art of Archetypal Psychology* (only available through Southwestern College). He has also worked extensively developing spiritual approaches to academic curriculum. He has a BA and MA in Sociology, an EdD in Educational Management and Development, is a licensed Mental Health Counselor in New Mexico, and founder and president of the Quimby Amenti Foundation.

PROLOGUE

"What's a mystic?" I asked Robert Waterman, my non-Catholic spiritual mentor one day. With no hesitation, he responded, "Merging with the mind and heart of Christ." *Quite Catholic*, I mused. Then sitting up straighter, he added, "We are all called to be mystics." Our conversation formed the inspiration for the title of the work you are now reading.

Before this conversation, whenever I thought of a mystic, I thought of Saint Teresa of Avila, or Saint John of the Cross, or Saint Francis of Assisi, Doctors of the Church, or my special friend, Saint Therese of Lisieux, who also has been pronounced a Doctor of the Church.

Many years ago, a psychic taught a class in my Hospice, Grief Counseling and Death education program. At the end of class Sandra Marie, the psychic, saw an image of St. Therese above me. She said she saw her put a rose on my heart. And after my mother died, several years later, I spent some time with Sandra Marie again, who told me that St. Therese helped my mother transition from life in this world to life in the next. Since then, I have considered St. Therese a special friend.

Mystics are the declared saints of the Catholic Church, who have been proven to have had visions, or levitated during prayer, and were able to be in total union with God at all times. After their deaths, each declared saint is expected to perform miracles approved by the Vatican in the lives of those who pray to them. Only then were people declared saints of the Catholic Church. Certainly, I did not think of myself—or all the other people that I know both in and out of my Religious Community—to be mystics or even to be called to mysticism.

I began to muse: *How would my life or any other person's life be different if I really "merged with the mind and heart of Christ?" What changes would I have to make? What beliefs would I have to change? What beliefs would I have to foster? Would family and friends look at me with skepticism? Where would this journey take me? Would I regret that I ever started on this path?* I would need much reflection on my life to respond to these questions.

My mind went back many years to a time when I was a young Religious (the term, Religious, in this sense means someone in a vowed religious community or order. In my case, this was the School Sisters of St. Francis). At that time, I was teaching in a small town in Iowa. One day, I looked up to the sky and said to God, "Teach me truth. Take me to the places I need to go and teach me the things I need to know so that I may find truth." At the time, I did not really know what I was asking, but I knew that it was a sacred moment.

As I look over my many years since that moment, I believe that God answered my prayer and "looked on me with love" as Jesus looked upon the young man in the Scriptures (Mark 10:21). God fulfilled my quest.

During the next sixty-plus years, my journey has taken me to new ministries; has given me opportunities to travel and learn in other countries; has introduced me to various groups and people unlike myself, from whom I learned much and often came to love; and has taken me to churches and synagogues and temples where I became acquainted with new and different ideas and rituals and beliefs that were not in my own background.

In all that time, God deeply loved and tenderly guided me through those hundreds of experiences that have helped to bring me to the truth of who I am—a child of God, a part of the Divine, a woman who knows the unconditional love of God. God truly listened and responds with love as I continue to search for truth!

The miracle in my life has been the recognition that this search goes on. It is an evolving process as I merge deeper into the mind and heart of Christ. It is the call and invitation of the Christ consciousness that resides deep inside each of us.

Introduction

n the early 1990s, after having shared my stories with others, several people urged me to record my stories in a book. After writing the first few chapters with input and suggestions from friends, I decided that I did not wish to finish it, and put it aside. Now, many years later, after I retired and moved to Milwaukee, God, the angels, or someone in the Spirit World would not let me alone. Each time I sat down to pray, and many times in between, I kept getting the urge to continue. Thus, it was necessary to pick it up again and finish it. But I would need to redo the finished chapters and basically start over. But who would help?

One night, I was visiting good friends, the Angeli family. I mentioned the book, which I felt needed to be written, and Liz's fiancée, Allen Brizee, spoke up and said, "I'll edit it for you." Allen is an English professor at Loyola University in Baltimore. He was willing to work with me gratis. What a gift! Now I knew this must be written.

The book is filled with true stories of experiences that took place over the course of my many years as a School Sister of St. Francis. Each of those stories became a springboard into a discussion of my belief system, my own searching and growth in the spiritual life. My hope is that my stories will inspire the reader of every religious affiliation, as well as others who are on a path of spiritual awakening, to examine the stories in his/her own life in search for the truth of "who they are." Each of us can recall those wonderful, and also difficult or tragic times, that can teach lessons of love and truth. May our stories assist each of us to "merge with the mind and heart of Christ" (God) in whatever lifestyle we have chosen.

I wrote this book more as a memoir than a biography. After chapter one, BEGINNINGS, which speaks about my childhood and my entry into the School Sisters of St. Francis, the rest of the chapters contain stories from various times in my life that set the stage for deeper reflection. Thus, they do not take the reader stage by stage along my life's path: rather they incorporate my life's path through experiences.

I think of my life in the School Sisters of St. Francis as 20-20-20. In three 20-year segments, I had the privilege of furthering our work and ministry in three different ways over the course of those sixty-plus years with a few extra years for a sabbatical and leadership roles.

The first twenty years, I spent teaching grade school in four Catholic Schools in the Midwest. Those years were filled with the excitement of learning to teach in a creative way. For the most part those years were happy and fulfilling. Two painful/stressful areas, which will be enlarged upon throughout the chapters were: 1) serious back trouble resulting in two surgeries, and 2) ministering for three years in one parish during which the Principal and I were far from understanding each other. These experiences became a new source of self-knowledge and openness to spiritual growth.

After earning a Master's Degree in Religious Education from Seattle University, and later a Sacred Theology Degree from Regis College in Toronto, Canada, I spent the second twenty years in several parishes, and in the diocesan offices of Des Moines, Iowa and Toledo, Ohio. Stories and incidences from these experiences are peppered throughout the chapters.

My third twenty years before retirement began in a most unique way: a deep felt urging that came from within, and could not be ignored. It was a call to go to Santa Fe, NM, where I was led to minister in hospice, grief counseling and death education.

Each chapter has the same basic format. At the beginning, I use a passage of Scripture to hint at the subject that will be considered. At the end of each chapter, I include a short reflection with suggestions that can be used for meditation. You may also choose to write out your answers to process your thoughts and feelings. Writing out your answers also provides you with a record of your thoughts and feelings that you may wish to return to later, and even add to if you are called to do so.

A model of written reflection that has been successful for others is the *What? So what? What now?* approach. This process is also known as "structured reflection." I included two different formats for the meditations. They say much the same. However, some readers may find quiet meditation more helpful, and others find writing more to their interest. It may be helpful to keep a journal handy for writing as well.

When answering the *What?* question, reflect on what you have done or what you are doing now that relates to the ideas I have discussed in the chapter.

When answering the *So what?* question, reflect on why these thoughts, events, or activities are meaningful to you.

When answering the *What now?* question, reflect and write about what you plan to do in the future to help resolve anything negative you may be experiencing that may be personally harmful or harmful to others— that is, steps you plan to take to resolve negativity in your life. You may also write about how you plan to resolve issues that are impeding your growth and path to God.

Lastly, you may want to reflect on how you might help others to grow closer to God.

It was significant for me to name each chapter with one word and then begin with a story. The book includes stories throughout to emphasize the experience and make the point I am trying to communicate. Every chapter with its stories and information has been helpful to my own growth, and perhaps to the readers as each of us continue to "merge with the mind and heart of Christ."

The first chapter, "Beginnings" introduces the reader to my childhood and the experience of love to which I was introduced through my family, my beloved horses and the School Sisters of St. Francis. In explaining my appreciation of nature and life in the thirties and forties, this chapter explains to the reader that a "little farm girl" from Iowa can learn new ways and follow God's call to an entirely new life as a School Sister of St. Francis.

I learned about the elements of intention from the Sisters in elementary school. Thus, Chapter, 2, "Intention," speaks about deepening my understanding and learning to use the energy of the Light of Christ for protection, both for myself and others for whom I wish to pray. Light casts out darkness and this chapter suggests ways of piercing darkness with Divine Light.

As I wrote the third chapter "Identity," I first looked at the Gospel of John and recognized how that Community who were followers of Jesus identified Him. In so doing, I realized the need to look closely at my own identity using my name in order to accept and appreciate who I am as an individual and yet as a beloved child of God.

I needed to write the chapter on "Harmony" because of the wonderful experiences I had had with certain teams in my ministry. I know well and have taught the Enneagram and the Chakras, which have become a large part of my understanding relationships with others as well as with my own self. Thus, I thought the reader might profit from an introduction to these two tools for understanding relationships in their own lives.

"Love," is a difficult but universal quality to understand. It is a deep hunger within everyone's heart. This chapter deals with human love and, with conscious awareness, may move the reader to recognize that the hunger for love is really a hunger for a deep connection with Infinite Divine Love. I also included this chapter because I believe, and have found, that love casts out fear, which may be helpful for readers as they engage on their spiritual journey.

Am I worthy? The chapter on "Worthiness," is about who Jesus is for me. Over the years, as I study the Jesus in history and the Christ of Faith, I am deepened by His teachings and His wisdom. May His life become the power that drives mine and, as I merge with his heart, I try to portray His in mine. We are all worthy since all are made in God's image.

The Divine presence has been a very unique part of my life. There is an abundance of stories that portray that reality. So as I wrote the chapter, "Presence," I recalled those stories and drew lessons to be learned. In my ministry, I learned how the Divine is present not only in my life, but in each and all of us. It was also a special privilege to experience God's presence from the Other Side.

The "Creativity" chapter explains that creativity is much more than various art forms. For much of my life, that was my concept, until I learned about my own creative ability beyond art. It was important to write about my discovery so that others also may find that deep interest within us to be creative in our lives and co-creators with our "Artist God."

I spent many years in the healing ministry and learned that everyone is in need of healing in body, mind, and/or spirit. The chapter, "Healing," shares with the reader that there are many kinds of grief. I felt that this was an opportunity to include some ideas and suggestions to help the reader process that pain if needed. My motto in teaching about death and loss is that "Grief is not a problem to be solved; rather it is a process whereby we can choose to become healthier and therefore holier."

Chapter 1

BEGINNINGS

Before I formed you in the womb I knew you
Before you were born I dedicated you.
(Jeremiah 1:5)

I was born and grew up on a small farm, in Fort Atkinson, Iowa, the third of four children. From the age of six or seven, I knew inside that I was to join the School Sisters of St. Francis in Milwaukee, Wisconsin. They were my grade school teachers and my inspiration.

There were always six Sisters. Four taught in the school, one was a musician, and one, a homemaker. I found them very kind and welcoming. Many Sunday afternoons when the family went to movies, or other places, I spent time with the Sisters doing little jobs or just talking and absorbing their presence. I got to know each of them and love them and I felt their love and care for me. They offered me a strong knowledge and faith in the Catholic Religion and silently encouraged my interest in Community. God's call was clearly running through my veins and enveloping my heart. I always felt much joy and acceptance being with those wonderful Sisters on those Sunday afternoons!

As a child at home, I spent several hours a day, at least during the summer, walking the fields of our farm, talking to our big work horses (they were my childhood "secret" keepers), and praying the rosary, novenas and other prayers. I never thought of myself as religious, and in those days, "spiritual" was not even in my vocabulary.

I loved the outside and spent much time with my Dad. When not in school, he and I spent hundreds of hours together talking about the farm, the animals, and about life itself. I was with him in the fields and with him on his cream route. I accompanied him as we did chores together, and I even proved to him that my hands were strong enough to milk the cows by hand. Milking machines were not common at that time, at least on small farms.

As I look back now, I realize that the reason I loved being with Dad was that he spoke to me as an adult. He would ask me about selling the hogs or buying or renting more land—things I knew nothing about as an elementary child. But I'm sure he made me feel important.

In the 1940s, small farmers were gradually modernizing, buying tractors and selling off their slow farm horses. I begged Dad not to sell our horses. They were my dearest friends and confidantes. Those big workhorses taught me unconditional love! They would stand by the fence for hours, while I petted them, and they listened to every word I said.

While I was still home, Dad honored my wishes, but after I left for the convent, he wrote one of his few letters telling me that he could no longer keep them. They followed him around the farm looking for me, and he could not stand it. I began to realize his dilemma; he had blessed my leaving, but it had deeply hurt my parents when they put me on that train and said "goodbye" to a beloved daughter who left them at thirteen.

Mom was quiet and thoughtful, yet kind and loving. She loved nature and music and was a wonderful cook, baker, and gardener; and she was very creative in all that she did. She loved to look over and admire the fields as the corn and oats grew. She loved and fed the birds and none of them ever went hungry. She provided houses for the wrens, her favorites, and enjoyed their beautiful songs.

Because it was so dark at night in the country, she loved to stand outside and admire the star-studded sky. I felt so comfortable being with her as she explained the Big and Little Dipper, the North Star, and other information she had about the sky. And she would recite the little poem, *Twinkle, twinkle little star, How I wonder where you are*—she had only an eighth grade education but seemed to know so much.

Mom also had a talent for music. She could hear a song once on the radio, and play the whole tune on the piano. After one year of music lessons, she was even able to read difficult music. She was often asked to play in church, and as Dad said, also at dances, while he became a wallflower. In addition to appreciating music, she also helped me appreciate nature—the trees, the landscape, the change of seasons, and the freedom of space on this small but nurturing farm.

I did not spend much time with Mom as a child, since I was outside with Dad most of the time. However, many years later, when I lived closer to home, I spent hundreds of hours discussing all aspects of life with her—she was in her eighties and nineties by that time. She told her stories of long ago. She had been the youngest of eleven, and her mother had died when she was twelve. It saddened me when she told me that she felt abandoned as a child.

Mom spoke about the difficulties her grandfather (whose wife had recently died in childbirth) had endured as he and the baby immigrated to the United States. Our discussion centered on religion, spirituality, sexuality, her fears about life after death, and much more. I was comfortable sharing all that with her. She was a treasury of wisdom and knowledge, and we shared deeply during the last days of her life. What joy Mom left with me!

Mom and Dad were not at all pleased to hear me talk about leaving for Milwaukee. I was thirteen, after all, and thirteen-year-old girls are supposed to begin high school, notice boys, and certainly not entertain dreams of entering a convent. At first, they teased me telling me that just like my older sister, June, who also spoke of convent life and was now married and living in Denver—I would soon forget about it.

My brother, Gene, was sure that I would only last two weeks in the convent, and my younger sister, Ethel, said little but seemed mystified and quiet as the discussion went on. I am sure she was sad, confused, and perhaps angry as the time grew closer, and she knew how much she would miss me. After all, I was her older sister, and I had taken care of her. We had spent our child-hoods together, had walked to school each day together, played together, finished household chores together, and like all siblings, had our little spats. We were close to each other in age, yet very different. But we were still sisters and fond of each other.

As we grew into adulthood, my sister Ethel and I became very good friends, and I deeply treasure our times together before death took her at age 60. So in the midst of all those feelings on the part of all of our whole family, I continued to insist that I leave after grade school and attend High School in St. Joseph Convent in Milwaukee, Wisconsin.

When Mom could not convince me to stay home by promising me a new watch, she pleaded with me to go to a convent closer to home. After all, there were several convents in Iowa and a few in Wisconsin that were much closer than Milwaukee. But at thirteen, as in so many future times in my life, I just knew what I had to do. I had to leave for St. Joseph Convent in Milwaukee, which was the one to which I was called to enter. So amidst pleading, cajoling and tears, I was finally given permission to leave. My desire was strong, but I remember taking off my brown slacks, which I had begged for (girls wore dresses in those days), hugging them and crying. Of course, no one, not even Mom, was privy to that.

Mom and Dad then took me to Calmar, Iowa, a small town four miles from Fort Atkinson, to catch the train that would take me to Milwaukee. It was a sad parting as they watched me, a young girl, their daughter, who felt the call of God. Yet, I knew that I had to leave my dear parents, my brother, my sister, and my beloved horses to venture into a totally unknown world. Thus, I felt excited, frightened, and sad when my eighth-grade teacher, Sister Meinharda, and I boarded the train that would take us on a twelve-hour trip, stopping, it seemed, in every small town the train tracks took us through Iowa and Wisconsin.

It was August 19, 1946.

Where did that strength come from? What meaning did this experience have for me? Why was I called at such a young age? How could I betray and sadden my parents like this? Where was God in all this pain for them? The questions have been with me throughout the years, and now as I write this book, some of those questions are being answered.

I had never been out of the state of Iowa. As the noisy train shook and rattled along the way, I noticed some change in the land-scape. The fields were getting ready for harvest—toward the end of August, the corn was turning brown and drying up so that the farmers could take in their bounty.

Many small towns dotted the landscape along the way. And every time we would stop, many people would get off and on. Everyone rode the train in those days. There were few planes, and little towns needed to be served.

I had never been on a train before. The shaking and wobbling and noise were new to me, but I was content being with Sister Meinharda and interested in all that was going on. I noticed the names of those little towns as we traveled along. Ossian, Postville, Monona. We rode through the bluffs as we neared the Mississippi River: McGregor—and then we crossed the river into Wisconsin—Prairie du Chien. It was exciting to cross the river. The Mississippi was as huge as imagined when we had studied it in our Iowa history course.

All the while, the train was taking me farther and farther from my family and home. Now, in the State of Wisconsin I remember noting unfamiliar town signs like Platteville,

Dodgeville, Madison, and finally, we arrived in Milwaukee.

Sister Meinharda was very attentive. I'm sure she was worried that I would be lonesome and want to go back. When we finally walked through the door of that huge Motherhouse, known as St. Joseph Convent, a feeling came over me that I will never forget. Peace and a calm contentment rose up inside me. I knew I was home! At thirteen, it felt awesome!

Thus, I began a totally new life and a new journey of getting to know God in a new way as an unconditional Lover and my Personal Guide struggling daily to "merge with the mind and heart of Christ."

REFLECTION

Spend some time remembering your childhood and your life as a young adult. Reflect on your chosen vocation, career, and way of life. What are some of the situations, the experiences, the feelings, the regrets, the fears, the joys that come to you?

Was your home happy? Did you feel safe, accepted, loved and cared for? Was there arguing, violence, abuse, addiction? Was there poverty, wealth? Was it religious or non-religious? Was there prejudice, judgment, gossip? Were there issues no one would discuss? What did you learn to appreciate or choose not to imitate? What belief systems were you taught?

SUGGESTION

Become aware of how your situations and experiences affected you as you got older. Identify the feelings connected with each of those times. Spend some time in gratitude or self-forgiveness. Ask forgiveness of another if that is appropriate. Speak to a counselor or spiritual guide or a friend if you feel stuck or unable to move into a space of joy. Honor yourself for the growth that has already taken place in you. Connect with God as you are guided.

WRITING OPTION

What? After reflecting on your childhood and young adult life, write about some of your most important memories with your family or friends and relations who mentored or guided you. What are some of the situations, the experiences, the feelings, the regrets, the fears, the joys that come to you? Was your home happy? Did you feel safe, accepted, loved and cared for?

Was there arguing, violence, abuse, addiction? Was there poverty, wealth? Was it religious or non-religious? Was there prejudice, judgment, gossip? Were there issues no one would discuss? What did you learn to appreciate or choose not to imitate? What belief systems were you taught?

So What? Write about why mentors were meaningful for you. Why did these people or memories come to you when reflecting about your early life? What about your upbringing and young adult life made these people or experiences so meaningful?

What Now? After reflecting and writing about early life experiences, you may have encountered some events that fill you with joy or that upset you. Write about how you intend to share or pass on joyful feelings with others, or write about how you intend to forgive or practice self-forgiveness for memories that upset you.

Write about the feelings you may feel stuck on; this may help you speak to a counselor or spiritual guide or a friend if you feel unable to move into a space of joy. You may also write about the progress you have made in the growth that has already taken place in you. Lastly, you may write about how you plan to connect with God as you are guided.

Chapter 2

INTENTION

Whatever you ask in my name
I will do so to glorify the Father in the Son.
(John 14:13)

s a young child, I learned about intention from the Sisters in my school. Each morning, the class would stand and recite the Morning Offering before lessons began. In this morning prayer, we offered our prayers, works, joys and sufferings, and our very lives in union with the Mass which, we were told, is offered in some place at all times throughout the world as a continuation of Jesus' Sacrifice on the Cross.

Over the years, the prayer got left behind, but intention—why I do things—has not diminished. In fact, it has become more real and important in my life.

The word *intend* as defined in the *Merriam Webster's Collegiate Dictionary,*

Tenth Edition, means to direct one's thoughts or faculties, to hear, to understand, to turn one's attention to, to have in mind as a purpose or goal. Having intention in what we do gives us hints on how we can extend our lives, and thereby, touch the lives of others and even our entire world.

Many articles and books have been devoted to the importance of intention during the last twenty years. Intention has been called attraction, i.e., attracting to ourselves what we really wish for or need. It has been called creating your own experience— abundance or health, or holiness or any other desire we may have.

As an example, *New York Times* best-selling authors, Esther and Jerry Hicks, have written several books on this topic, *The Law of Attraction, Ask and It Is Given,* and *The Amazing Power of Deliberation.* They also have cards and CDs. I have seen prayer cards and short articles on this same topic. Thus, some authors even tell us that intention creates our own reality. So can it?

Intention was not in my thought as I said to God that day long ago, "Teach me truth." I now know that my intention was powerful. It was a strong plea, a desire that enveloped my whole being as I experienced it on the physical level as well as in my soul. My entire being participated in that prayer. And I am convinced that God listened and granted my petition; for the many years of experiences that followed, my life taught me truth in ways I could never have imagined.

For intention to really be meaningful, it is important to look at the whole process. We may wish for something that forms in our thought, but the wish cannot stay there. It must move intently into our feelings, into our heart's desire. The will must then take over and push us to perform the action to do whatever it takes to accomplish that wish. As humans, we often keep intention only as thought and go no further. Thought, feeling, and action are all part of the process.

When I make the intention and consciously choose to be compassionate, loving or giving as I go about my ordinary life, I find that I make many mistakes, or as some writers say, *I am missing the mark*. However, that conscious intention made earlier more easily brings me back to myself to again strive to be that loving person I intend to be. Distractions and mistakes are to be used as teaching guides to let go of the negative ego and keep centered on what is really important. For me, this planet is one great big classroom whereby we can choose to learn the lessons of love, which may at times be difficult, painful, or even tragic.

With intention, we can add our part, small or large, towards bringing peace into this world. We can indeed create transformation in ourselves, our place of work, problems in our city and in our country. Intention is a very powerful tool to incorporate into our prayer, as well as into our actions. When there is pain, difficulty, strife, or the need for healing, the process of intention must be part of prayer.

Several years ago, I was living in a large apartment complex. Because it was geared toward the lower income community, I decided to spend time each morning mentally going through the building, sending blessings to those who were willing to accept a blessing. I did not wish to be invasive, so as I prayed, I checked in psychically to recognize who would be willing to accept the blessing and who would not. My prayer was for the highest good for each one living there.

When I first moved in, I knew nobody in the building, but as I mentally went from apartment to apartment, I got the message that there was one person who would not accept this blessing. I knew instinctively who it was, so thereafter, each time our paths crossed, I greeted him cheerfully. After a while, I sensed that he psychically was willing to accept my intent for his highest good. It was strange, but real.

There were a few people in the building who had a drinking problem, and one day a young father spoke to me about one of them who was disturbing to him and his family. He feared that he would have to move. I intensified my prayers for his family and the person who was disturbing them. Several days later, the young husband elatedly told me that the person who had annoyed them had moved out, and soon two others followed. No one knew I was performing this action. Did the blessings I sent to each of those apartments have an impact on the people who lived there? Since my intention was to make the building more secure and healthy, I believe that it did.

The way I make my intention today is very different from the "morning prayer" I said as a child. My whole being, my thoughts, my emotions, and my loving heart must become conscious of my intention. I try to image what I wish for in my mind, and involve the physical, emotional, mental and spiritual parts of me. I then direct my intention to that particular need, lovingly and compassionately always with the intention for the highest good of all concerned.

As I do so, I invite the Light of Christ and the Light of the Holy Spirit to permeate every part of me—physical, emotional, mental, and spiritual—including my auric field of energy. (Everything is energy. Thus each of us has a field of energy around us, which is like an aura. This is also part of us). I then direct that Light to the person or persons or situation as much as they can receive it.

What do I mean by "the Light"?

The symbolism of Light is universal and has a place in all cultures and all religions.

Light has various meanings in the Christian Scriptures. It sometimes means the material sense of outward light or daybreak, as in Genesis when God created Light out of darkness, i.e., chaos (Genesis 1:3). It is also a symbol of God showing God's incorporeal, pure and holy nature as in 1 John 1: 5: "God is Light; in Him there is no darkness." It is very much a symbol of Christ in John 8:12: "I am the Light of the world. No follower of mine shall ever walk in darkness."

Christians are called the Children of Light because they have received the spiritual Light of truth and grace, and are encouraged to radiate this Light in the world by their good example. Matthew 5:14: "You are the Light of the world. A city set on a hill cannot be hidden." And finally, in Ephesians 5:8, we read, "There was a time when you were darkness, but now you are light in the Lord. Well, then live as children of Light."

In the New Testament, Light refers to the Godhead, to Jesus and to us Christians. Whether the story is about Peter in prison

(Acts 12:7) or Saul blinded by the Light on the way to Damascus (Acts 9:3), the illumination at the time of the Transfiguration (Luke 9:29-30), or the Light in the form of Angels surrounding Jesus' birth (Luke 2:9-14), Divinity is present in the form of angels, Mary, or Jesus Himself.

Light, however, is also identified with Life: "Whatever came to be in Him found life, life for the Light of men" (John 1:4). The 1967 edition of *A New Catechism* names John the Baptist the Witness to the Light, which, of course, is Christ. Scripture speaks of Light so often that for the Christian, the familiarity of it is sometimes taken for granted. Therefore, it is imperative that we recognize the Light as our Life, the breath of God, the way we are kept alive physically and spiritually.

A very dramatic understanding of the Light of Christ takes place for many Christian denominations, which follow the Eucharistic tradition—Catholics, Anglicans, Eastern Orthodox, and others—at the Easter Vigil on Holy Saturday Night. Each person who enters the church is given a small candle. During the ceremony that follows, the large

Easter candle is lit in the midst of many prayers, readings and ritual. All stand and hold a candle and are presented with the Light from the newly lit Easter candle. As the small candles are lit, the light grows larger and larger until the entire Church is filled with Light.

For me, this is a perfect symbol of intention as the dictionary explains it. Light stretches, strains, and directs its energy beyond itself. Just as the large Easter candle sends forth its Light, I, through intention, can send the Light of Christ (God) far beyond me into a special person, a Community, a World.

Christianity is only one faith that uses Light in so much of its ritual, prayer, and understanding; most other religions do also. Inner Light is essential to the Quaker Community. The Jewish Kabbalah speaks of the Divine as "light without end." The Koran, the sacred scripture of Islam, reads, "God is the Light of heaven and earth" (24:35). And in Buddhism and other traditions, Light and Enlightenment are central teachings.

As I write this, I have been asked to pray for a small child dying in a city many miles from here. She is not aware that I am praying for her. However, several times a day, I send her Light and energy. Since everything is energy in some form, I send her the energy that she needs to heal her body, and that energy flows to her to help her progress to the next stage in her journey to God. My intention always needs to be for her highest good and the highest good of those who love her. I do not know what that may be, but God and the Divine powers around her know. Then, I must trust that God will give healing to her body, mind and spirit as is her need.

Many years ago, I was living in Omaha, Nebraska, where there was a convent of Poor Clare Nuns. This order of nuns spends much time in prayer and silence. I was Provincial (Leader) of our Omaha Province at the time and became a friend of the Superior of the convent. She invited me to come as often as I could, to spend a quiet day in that holy place away from my work.

One day, on one of their feast days, I was invited to have a meal with the entire community. As I was speaking to one of the elderly nuns, she told me that before she goes to chapel for prayer, which is very early in the morning, she listens to the radio. Quite surprised, I asked her why. Her response was, "I need to know what and who to pray for during the day."

She went on to tell me that every day, she prayed for a certain person in Communist Russia, because she knew him to be a good man, and she felt he needed her prayer. Years later, the person for whom she prayed became a catalyst for bringing down the Iron Curtain. How much was the pure intention of this elderly nun in Omaha, Nebraska, part of change for the Soviet Union? Perhaps more than we realize. That day, I learned another connection between prayer and intention.

As I see myself as a being of Light united to the Christ Light, I feel that I get the strength I need to perform the work that I am called to do. Being in human form, our energy is finite; however, when we draw in the Light of Christ, we have resources of the Divine to be for the highest good of all.

For almost twenty years, my ministry was working in a funeral home as a grief counselor. Every day, I met people who were suffering, and very vulnerable, having recently experienced the death of a loved one. For them, I constantly strove to be a "lighted being." I learned how I could empathize without taking away their power to heal, how I could caution without advising, how I could be compassionate without pitying. As I looked into the eyes of those who were suffering intense loss, my intention was to be their strength and compassion, at least for a short time.

Hundreds of times, as I counseled people suffering from the death of a dear family member or friend, I encouraged them to intentionally surround themselves and their loved one with the Light of the Christ and the Holy Spirit in order to gain comfort and peace.

As part of my ministry, I facilitated a support group for the men and women whose spouses had died. I often spoke to them about inviting in the Light to surround them for healing and intentionally to place their loved one in the Light as well.

Each time I spoke of the Light and its protection, an older man who was Christian, but not of the Catholic denomination, teased me and let me know that he believed it was a foolish practice. He would say things like, "Oh, you and the Light! That's crazy." He did so jokingly, but I knew that he thought the practice was nonsense. I met him a few years later. His health had deteriorated severely, and he worried about his own death. He looked at me and said, "Now, I know what you mean by the Light. I use the practice and it helps me. I can be more calm and accepting of my problems."

Around 1986, I was just beginning my ministry in the Toledo Diocese as part of a team of religious education coordinators for the fifty Catholic parishes in Toledo, Ohio. This was a totally new city for me. I was nervous and found myself stewing inside about the unknown, especially getting lost in a new city.

In the midst of my stewing, and with no warning, I heard my nephew, who had been killed at age 21 in 1974 say loudly within me, "Don't worry, Arlene, I will take care of you."

Surprised, I stopped my worrying. I knew that Gene had excelled in his knowledge of cars, so I trusted him to get me to wherever I needed to go. And he came through wonderfully. When I needed help, I would talk to him, and he would be there. Whenever I found myself lost or in an unfamiliar place, I would ask for his guidance (I had already put the Light around my car), and in no time, I would recognize a familiar street or road sign and easily get out of the situation. It was amazing!

Remembering is the difficulty. It is much easier to get upset, stew and worry about the problem, and then go on with life, forgetting the help that is always available. How often I forget about my connection with the Divine and fail to recognize that Divinity wishes to be part of my minute-to-minute life. Yet, the more I practice setting my intention to connect with the Divine, the more I discover that God's intentions become what I intend. With this deeper connection, the flow of Light brings me closer to the One.

Writers of sacred literature and spirituality try to explain our connection to the Divine through symbolism and images. Some say that each of us in the human family is a spark of God or a wave in the ocean of Divine love. Images create a reality by which we can grasp meaning and live by it. When Jesus says, "I am the true vine, and my Father is the vine grower...No more than a branch can bear fruit of itself apart from the vine, can you bear fruit apart from me. I am the vine, you are the branches" (John 15:1-5), or when He called Himself "the Bread of Life": "I, myself, am the Bread of Life." (John 6:35), we recognize images upon which to better understand our Divine connection. And every Catholic child who attends a Catholic school or a Religious Education program is taught that we are made in the image and likeness of God.

The belief that we, as humans, came from the Divine and are seeking to return to the realms of Light may create varied images, but the truth of "who we are" as part of God, remains the same. We are made in God's image and likeness. We are a breath of God. We are a Divine spark, and God looks upon us and loves each of us individually. We are that wave in the ocean of Divine Love.

We know from the writings of many authors that Light, as well as everything else in our universe, is energy. To touch into that energy of subtle Light is very powerful. The Light, the Christ consciousness, the Universal energy, the Holy Spirit—whatever we may call it, is part of this entire cosmos. It is also in everyone, Christians and non-Christians alike—the entire human family. It is our birthright, whether or not we recognize it.

The Light is our support and our lifeline. When we become aware of its power and move deeply into our consciousness, we can feel it in several ways. When the energy is strong, some people feel a tingling, a chill, or warmth. Many times those feelings are ignored or thought of as vivid imagination. In reality, those feelings may be energy surging through the body connecting us with the Divine.

Many years ago, as I was speaking to my spiritual director about the phenomenon of strong energy, I said, "This is just my imagination."

His response was, "Is imagination real?"

Imagination is as real as the mind and the body, and like the mind, as well as the body, it is available for our use in meditation and prayer. As an example of using the imagination in meditation, one can invite in the Light, read a story from Scripture, or a passage from other inspirational texts, or even watch a movie and imagine ourselves as one of the characters. How has this character lived life? How would I have lived it a different way? How can I look deeply into my own spiritual life and connect with my higher self, with God, with the Divine? Can I take this character and use the story line to become a person of greater depth or to move closer to living in higher consciousness and with a deeper awareness of life around me?

As we connect with the Divine, we may feel energy move through us and overwhelm us with gratitude or forgiveness or unconditional love. Thus, over the years, I have come to recognize the strength of energy in various forms. I have recognized the power of energy that comes from the Light and the power of imagination that helps me to meditate. And I have recognized that our whole being can connect us with the Divine.

When I set the intention and invite the Light to work with me, it is important to remember to invite, not to demand. I must do so with humility. I am not greater than or less than anything or anyone else. God is not my Servant. God's unconditional love responds to a gentle invitation. Our love and desire to grow deeper into being one with God is the special gift of God.

I need to make a note here. Intention can be misused. Freedom is a choice to be used for good or for evil. Intention begins with belief. If we believe that we can hurt others, and intend to do so, the energy that we send to them is negative and can be harmful.

When we send out negative energy through our anger or fear or hatred, it is as powerful as sending out good and holy energy to a person or situation. Thus, it is important to remember that energy is powerful and can be used as a gift for good or for evil intent. May our thoughts and the energy that we send to others always be wrapped in the Light of the Holy Spirit!

REFLECTION

Recall many needs of our world: peace, the alleviation of hunger, the cessation of war in any part of our world, the injustice of the prison system, the death penalty, torture, those contemplating abortion, murder, or suicide, the destruction of the environment, or any other evil or need of our country or our planet.

SUGGESTION

This suggestion can be done alone or with an interested group, which would be more powerful. For Jesus said, "Again I tell you, if two or three of you join your voices on earth to pray for anything whatever, it shall be granted you by my Father in heaven. Where two or three are gathered in My name, there am I in the midst of them" (Matthew 18:19-20).

Decide upon a certain area of need that the group is open to pray about. Invite the Christ Light, the Angels, and any other Beings from the Highest Realms to participate with you if they choose to be part of this time together. Thank them for coming. Then, with the power of intention and as a group, ask the Light to pierce the darkness of each or some of the above needs. Let the energy flow as the group, or within yourself, and create healing images in areas of need.

WRITING OPTION

What? After finishing this chapter, recall some of the darkness in our world: war, poverty, fear, ignorance, prisons, torture chambers, refugee camps, homeless, violence, greed, power and sex abuse, the hopelessness surrounding the need for abortion, euthanasia, suicide, the destruction of the environment, and any other injustice of which you may be aware in our country and our planet.

Reflect and write about the following questions: What feelings come to the surface for you? Do you look upon the problems with despair? Do you feel helpless about changing them? Is there a feeling of powerlessness?

So What? Spend some time praying and thinking about the pain around us. Because we are all ONE, recognize that we also are part of the pain. Invite the Spirit world, angels, the Christ, God, Holy Spirit or anyone who may be willing to assist in the healing of this problem or any particular one that may attract you at this time. Write about why this is meaningful for you. Why do you think it is important to address the pain of the world?

What Now? This suggestion can be done alone or with an interested group, which would be more powerful. For Jesus said, "Again I tell you, if two or three of you join your voices on earth to pray for anything whatever, it shall be granted you by my Father in heaven. Where two or three are gathered in My name, there am I in the midst of them" (Matthew 18:19-20).

Decide upon a certain area of need that the group is open to pray about. Invite the Christ Light, the Angels, and any other Beings from the Highest Realms to participate with you if they choose to be part of this time together. Thank them for coming. Then, with the power of intention and as a group, ask the Light to pierce the darkness of each or some of the above needs. Let the energy flow as the group or within oneself and create healing images in areas of need.

Write about what you feel during this process. How do you intend on using the Christ Light, Angels, or Beings from the Highest Realms to help you address some of the pain you notice around you?

Chapter 3

IDENTITY

I AM the Bread of Life (John 6:48)
I AM the Light of the World (John 8:12)
I AM the Gate (John 10:9)
I AM the Good Shepherd (John 10:11
  and 14)
I AM the Resurrection and the Life
  (John 11:26)
I AM the Way the Truth and the Life
  (John 14:6)
I AM the True Vine (John 15:1)

The seven I AM statements above, found in John's Gospel, speak to Jesus' identity. The community for whom John was writing believed that these statements describe who Jesus is.

I am the Bread of Life, the sustenance by which we are kept alive. All life from plants to humans cannot live without some sort of sustenance. That image, together with the other I AM images, speaks to what that Community believed identified the Jesus whom they loved.

I am the Light. Jesus takes us out of the darkness of sadness, selfishness, evil, sin, depression, and any other darkness in our lives. But He also says I am the Light of the World. He promises to bring this world also into the Light of peace that is Divine.

I am the Gate. The gate is open. We are invited to enter it and be free. Jesus will not close the gate and leave us to ourselves. Rather, His gift is an open gate giving us the freedom to move in and out as we choose. His identity is freedom!

I am the Good Shepherd. A shepherd is not part of our ordinary life today. However, the message for me in this image is total dependence. Sheep are in constant need of the shepherd to lead. Jesus takes the lead for those of us who wish to follow Him.

I am the Resurrection and the Life. This image for me is not rising on the last day, as our Church teaches, but rising with Him each day, doing our ordinary duties in relationship with others through kindness and love.

I am the Way, the Truth and the Life. Jesus is my way as I strive to listen to His teachings and BE him in my world. He has been my truth answering my petition of long ago. And He is my life as I live it daily for Him.

I am the vine. As the branches cling to the vine, I must cling to His teachings, His love, His insights, and His whole Being.

When John's Gospel was written, Jesus was no longer present in human form. In order for that Community to know and understand His presence among them now, the author used symbols and images. In meditating upon those images, the Community would have a means by which they could understand the wisdom that Jesus left with them and apply those teachings to their own lives.

Authors who write about the spiritual life emphasize the importance of knowing ourselves, knowing our true identity, becoming aware of "who we are" before God. As you move through this book and choose to use the meditations and/or writing exercises at the end of each chapter, you may clarify your own identity and use that knowledge to recognize gifts, and virtues, as well as the behavior and motivations that keep you from a deeper connection with the Divine.

Gently holding and appreciating our own identity can lead us more deeply into "merging with the mind and heart of Christ."

Why do I believe "identity" is so important so early on in this book? For many years, as I counseled people, I heard many say, "I don't know who I really am. What is my purpose in life? I am confused about who I am and what I should be doing. What does God really want of me?" I recognized poor self-esteem in so many of those whom I have counseled. For many years, I had some of those same questions.

Then one day, I got an insight into knowing and understanding the importance of identity through my name. It helped me to know myself in a more wholesome way and to grow in my own self-esteem. Perhaps some of my insights and stories will encourage you to seek a deeper identity about who you are.

I was sitting in a kiva, a Pueblo Indian ceremonial structure built under ground and in a circular fashion, in northern New Mexico, as part of a pipe ceremony facilitated by a woman who had been trained by a shaman. The weekend had been very powerful. Three of us—Melissa Pickett, Naneki Elliott, and I—had just finished facilitating a retreat called "The Love, Will, and Wisdom of the Divine Feminine," which we had prepared over the course of several months. We three and the seven who had made the retreat had moved deeply into the experience of recognizing the Divine Feminine within our own being and the kiva ceremony was the culmination.

Through the ritual of the pipe ceremony, the leader included many prayers and blessings for the group. She made holy the work each participant had finished during the retreat. We were now prepared to go back to our own lives.

Suddenly, and without warning, I felt the presence of two School Sisters of St. Francis: Sister Meinharda, my dear eighth-grade teacher, and Sister Judea, my principal, whom I dearly loved during my first years of teaching at St. William's Chicago. Both had died many years before, yet I felt the energy of their presence in the kiva as if they were sitting next to me in bodily form. They gave me a very important message. "Arlene, you need to go back over the years when you were Sister Linda and heal from those experiences." The message was clear, and the reason for it was very important.

I began to realize then the importance of names. For instance, what happens inside a woman whose name is Jane Doe, and upon marriage, becomes Mrs. John Smith or the thousands of women in religious communities being assigned a name very different from the name given at birth or Baptism? And sadly, many of those names were male, and many difficult, unattractive, and often made fun of by the children in the classrooms.

God, in the Christian Scriptures, seemed to realize the importance of names. In Genesis 2:22, we read: "The man gave names to all the cattle, all the birds of the air and all the wild animals." In Genesis 17, as God was making a covenant of circumcision with Abram, asking him to walk in God's presence and be blameless, God said in verse 5, "No longer shall you be called Abram; your name shall be Abraham."

Jesus also changed Simon, the name of one of His apostles, to Peter. In Luke 6:13-14, we read: "At daybreak he called his disciples and selected twelve of them to be his apostles: Simon, to whom he gave the name Peter…" And in John 1:42, we read: "He, Andrew, brought him to Jesus, who looked at him and said, "You are Simon, son of John: your name shall be Cephas (which is rendered Peter)."

The experience of my name Arlene being changed to Sister Linda happened when I entered the Novitiate on June 13, 1949 with sixty-four other novices. During that ceremony, each novice was given a new name by the Mother General of the School Sisters of St. Francis. This ritual was very significant and had a very deep meaning, for we were not only to assume a different name; we were now beginning a new life, and were to leave the old one behind. So as I received the habit of the School Sisters of St. Francis, my name was changed from Arlene to Sister Linda and my new identity was that I was now to prepare to become a "Bride of Christ."

As I knelt at the communion railing, Mother Corona approached each novice, giving out her new name. I was very nervous. What name would I receive? Would it be what I had asked for? Would it be one my parents would accept? Would it be one that I could live with or would it be strange and ugly? I tried to be accepting.

Then I heard, "Your name in religion will be Sister Mary Linda. Strive to bear it in a worthy manner." I was relieved. It was the first of the three names for which I had asked, named after my oldest niece. Each novice had the name "Mary" in her name in honor of Mary the Mother of Jesus. I was fortunate to be given the lovely name, Linda, a feminine name and one that means "beautiful" in Spanish. Sister Linda was to be my name for about twenty years!

As I look back on the experience of that ritual and have learned about the universality and the power of energy, I recognize that energy or the vibration in a name says a lot about our identity.

Science has proven that everything in the universe is some kind of energy—even God.

The first time I heard that, perhaps forty years ago, I was shocked and doubtful. However, I now know it is true and that all things are ONE. Everything vibrates at its own pace—even words. As an experiment, say harsh words aloud, such as anger, murder, hatred, war, and so on, and then gentle words such as kind, loving, compassion, gentle, tenderness, and so on, and note the difference.

Now, many years later, through my two wonderful friends who spoke to me in the kiva, I needed to reflect upon the identity I had assumed so many years before. What experiences had I encountered during those twenty years that needed to be healed? What were some of the happenings that needed reflection and perhaps even retelling the stories to a friend, a counselor or a spiritual mentor in order to bring forward the sadness, the anger, the guilt or any other feelings that may still be buried in the depth of my being? Had I not really let them go? Was now the time to do so?

As I began to take stock of those days of being Linda, I felt that I needed to go back even farther—all the way to childhood—to note what is in a name. How does a name connect with one's identity?

My second name is Eva, a name that I never liked and when people asked what my second name was, I usually avoided the answer and, most of the time, succeeded to keep the name secret.

Since then I learned that the name Eva, according to metaphysical teachings, refers to the feminine aspect of the Divine in Creation. It recalls the tears in the birthing of human life. How beautiful! Also the name Eva, taken from the Hebrew has another beautiful meaning—*life, the living one, full of life.* That name fits me well.

Now, many years later, as I contemplate my second name, I believe that my parents were inspired to name me Eva (no one else in the family has it) so that it could help me to remember my background—a farm girl sur-rounded by life in nature, who from early childhood, spent many hours connecting with the Divine as she walked through the fields. It has put me in touch with my true essence as part of God and is causing me to remember that we as humans, birthed often through tears, are connected to all of creation and not separate as the human family needs to become. It is a call to live in higher consciousness, which is learning to replace the part of the negativity within the ego to live with deeper insight, awareness, intuitive understanding, and love. For me, it is a call to "birth" human life through compassion, gentleness, and loving kindness. So, my second name has become a new reminder of the unity of the human family, and in reality, of all creation.

However, those beautiful thoughts were not in my consciousness as a child. As I check into the vibration of the name, I always thought of myself more of an Arlene than an Eva. Eva is a demure name and perhaps at home, I fit the pattern for I was quite serious, reserved, and shy, especially around others. I had no reason to "rock the boat." As said earlier, I spent as much time in nature with my dad as I was able, going with him on his cream route, helping to repair telephone lines, fixing fences, milking cows, or working with the animals. Dad and Mom each in their own way put me in touch with nature. So, although I did not like the name, Eva, it seemed to fit during that time in my life.

The root meaning of Arlene is "strong," which is explained in a little book published by *Our Sunday Visitor, Saints for Girls, A Saint for Your Name,* by Albert J. Nevins, M.M. (1980). Arlene is the feminine version of Charles, Teutonic: strong.

In school, I was much more assertive and the "Arlene" came out quite strongly. I was a good student and took on some of the leadership positions. Because of small classes and excellent teachers, I was able to foster abilities that I did not realize I had. I was compulsive, and because of that behavior, my eighth grade teacher called me "Peter" after the compulsive Peter, one of the disciples of Jesus. Even as children, we assume new identities in different situations.

Most of my teenage years were spent in the Convent and then I became much more of an "Arlene". Very soon after I arrived at St. Joseph Convent in Milwaukee, I found myself with a very different identity. I changed quickly and drastically. I became quite noisy, talkative, independent, and therefore I always seemed to be in trouble with the leadership. The first directors I had in the Community brought out the worst in me and the strong name of "Arlene" began to show itself. I asserted my independence and some teenage rebelliousness, much to the frustration of my Superiors. The "Arlene" in me lasted until I was given the name "Linda" when I became a novice in 1949.

Being in novitiate as a School Sister of St. Francis became a haven for me. There were two large groups of us—about 120 in all. Besides prayer and Mass, the first-year novices spent most of their time learning about Religious Life and the study of religion and spirituality. We were also partly responsible for cleaning and food preparation in the huge St. Joseph Convent. Our jobs were also to help with the hundreds of loads of laundry. The second-year novices spent most of their time in college, preparing for the ministry of teaching, nursing, music, missionary work, or whatever else they were called to do after taking their vows.

During those days, I contemplated what it meant to become a "Bride of Christ." I found it to be a very heavy burden to carry. The life of Jesus as we know it through the New Testament began as ordinary—learning new skills and knowledge, perhaps from the Essenes and studying in the East, but still doing the ordinary things of life. However, His adult life then took a new turn. It became filled with the wisdom of His teaching, the miracles of healing the sick and counseling the poor of His day. He performed miracles of nature and blessed with deep love those around Him. His life at the end became very difficult, and His Resurrection culminated a life that I certainly felt I could not imitate. We call Him the Christ—the Anointed One. How could I be the "Bride" of the Anointed One?

What does it really mean to be the "Bride of Christ"? Jesus is always with us as a friend, a beloved, a mentor, a teacher, or in any way we need Him to be at any given moment but most of all He is an example of how to live life. By His example, Jesus taught us who God, His and ours, Father/Mother really is—the God of infinite love, not the punitive God of the Old Testament.

Anyone who strives to learn the wisdom of living in conscious awareness and practice His teachings is connected to Him in a deep and lasting way. The deep love He has for those around Him is the call of all those who strive to be holy as God is holy. Perhaps that is when any of us—or all of us—becomes the "Bride of Christ."

So what did those two Sisters who came to me in the kiva wish for me when they told me that I needed to heal from the time I began my life as "Linda?"

"Linda" is a much softer name with a very different vibration from "Arlene." As I look back over those years, I sense that I was much more vulnerable and even fragile. In the novitiate, I did not feel the need to struggle with my Novice Director. She was fair and kind. I found myself open to her teachings. Was it the new identity of the name? Or was it her goodness that touched me, thus helping me to settle into the process of becoming the best that I could become? Perhaps it was both.

My first assignment was a shock—to teach second grade in a large Catholic school in Chicago. I had come from a small town in Iowa. Chicago was huge! How could I ever adjust to Chicago? As I had been looking towards an assignment to a teaching position, I said to God, "Send me anywhere but NOT to Chicago." My wish certainly was not granted, and the joke expressed by my friends and me many times over the course of the years was, "If you wish to make God laugh, plan." In my case, this was surely true! My journey had already been planned, and the Chicago chapter in my life became a wonderful experience.

St. William Parish was the place where I was best suited to begin my teaching career. In truth, God knew what S/He was doing, and though I began my ministry with feelings of fear, and insecurity, it was a new and exciting time. I was very young and learned fast. At the age of eighteen, I had enthusiasm and great expectations!

In those days, when teaching in large Catholic schools, it was common to have fifty or sixty children to a grade. I had fifty-four lively little second graders. The first year was very difficult, as I had to learn by trial and error. How quickly one learns to become creative in the face of difficulty! But after two years, I had settled into teaching and experienced much joy.

Then the third year, Sister Judea, the wonderful principal who met me in the kiva, arrived and for the next six years she inspired me, gave numerous ideas for teaching, and became a wonderful friend. I found myself happy and contented.

Our group of twenty-one Sisters enjoyed one another, had lots of fun despite our many duties, and I came into my own as an excellent teacher. During the nine years I spent in Chicago, I found my new identity as an educator and a leader in promoting self-directed learning. I loved the children whom I taught, and they loved me. So even with those large numbers, the children learned and progressed in my busy classroom.

In the midst of these growth-filled and wonderful years of teaching the little ones, the time of trial was at hand. My back "went out" and in those days, with no MRI to discover the cause, doctors were at a loss to understand why I was experiencing such awful pain. Fear, confusion, and the responsibility I felt for my classes took over.

It was a period of extreme uncertainty. How could I continue teaching with this amount of pain? Would I ever be pain-free, or is this the life I will have to the end? What is this pain about and what am I to learn from it?

So that I could be treated by a back specialist closer to St. Joseph Convent, I was assigned to another large school in Milwaukee, St. Rita's. The back specialist in Milwaukee was able to provide some relief by giving me a back brace.

At St. Rita's, I became part of a different group of Sisters and was scheduled to teach eighth-grade students. Eighth grade became my favorite grade, and I enjoyed the energy and creativity of that age level. The four of us eighth-grade teachers worked together very well, and I began to learn to work as a team.

The Superior/Principal at this school, however, did not understand me or my gifts for teaching and guiding the older students. As a result, I lost my voice for speaking my own truth. During those three years at St. Rita's, I relied on my eighth-grade students and the team of my fellow teachers to bring security and joy into my life. Again, an identity change as I learned to live with physical and psychological pain!

It took a total of ten years of severe pain and struggle before two surgeries contributed to the healing of my back.

Pain is a catalyst for change. It can make us holier or push us into despair. These are the times that we can choose to grow or choose to become a victim. Using the graces God gave me, I became much more mellow, sensitized, gentle, loving, and confident in myself. Now, I needed to find another new identity—one without pain, but one that caused me to also be more gentle with myself. This, of course, takes a lifetime of work and reliance on God. I am still working and will be until I make my transition.

It was during those years when my name was Linda that I learned to love in a human way and learned to accept the principal from whom I got no support. I also took on various leadership positions within and outside of my Religious Community at the very difficult time when Vatican II was on the horizon. I then began to reflect upon how different roles and careers make deep changes in our lives as we try to adjust to the journey our life has taken us.

My reflections took me beyond my own life and the major changes that everyone encounters through the roles that we take on or the hats that we wear as we move through one chapter after another in our lives.

Who must a person become as she takes the name of Mrs. Smith on her wedding day, or Sister Linda on Reception Day, or Ms. Jones, on the day she begins a career after college? Who really is nun, or mother, or father, or husband, or wife, or professor, or farmer, or politician, or businessman or business woman, and which hat does one wear without falling prey to identity confusion?

Am I an independent professional on one level and an immature child on another? Am I able to do well in a job during the day and sink into an addiction in the evening? Do I handle my relationships well in my professional life and then come home and become uncommunicative, sullen, angry or even violent with my spouse and/or children or the Sisters with whom I live? Am I "alive" with my peers in the workplace and become a couch potato with no initiative at home? What am I to learn as I look at the role I play in life?

Each situation has its own story, and through all of my experiences, I felt challenged and was given the opportunity to grow and change from situation to situation. As each difficult situation arose along with the confusion that comes with it, I was very fortunate to have wonderful support from many friends from within and outside my Community. Now, after all these years, I was invited to take the advice from my "kiva Sister friends" and learn that healing can take place many years later and that it is an ongoing process. I recognize that our identity is always in constant flux! And our work is to learn what our core, our essence, our God image is inside and to grow from that place.

Everyone struggles with identity. We wear masks; we play games; we create our own agenda. We identify with our job, or our career. We believe our importance is identified with the amount of money we possess or the raise that we were given. We identify with the education that we have or the knowledge that we possess. For many of us, our identity depends upon the clothes we wear or the car that we drive.

But identities can change and often we change with them.

Vatican II happened from between 1962 and 1965. Many changes occurred in the church, as Catholics know well. Religious Sisters had their own directive. We were asked by Rome to go back to the beginning of our Communities and to study the vision and mission of our foundresses. One very important motto of our foundress, Mother Alexia, was, "The needs of the time are the will of God for us." She also said, "The word, 'impossible' is a word I do not know." These messages spoke to all of us.

To meet the needs of the times, we needed to change much of our lifestyle. We needed to become more of a part of the communities we served. We changed our dress, we changed our structure, we studied the deeper meaning of our vows, and we were given permission to change our names back to our baptismal names if we chose to do so. Some Sisters did and some chose not to do so. I was urged to do so, particularly by a friend who told me I was more of an "Arlene" than a "Linda." I realize how right she was. After I did so, I noted that I gradually became stronger.

When I changed my name back to Arlene after about twenty years, I understood that I had become stronger, more secure and confident within myself. Again, how much does it have to do with the vibration of the name or growth in maturity? I think both!

To some extent, our identity does depend upon our family origin, our race, our sexual orientation, our religion, our political leanings, and all those parts of us that we show to the world and to others who know us. This is our ego. However, those are all external aspects of the individual and have varying degrees of importance and just a very small part of our real identity, our core, our true Self. In this process, we learn who we are in the deepest part of our being, and we struggle to get beyond the outside influences.

I believe that the most important work we have to do in this lifetime is to develop an intimate connection with the Divine, who is as close to us as our breath. For me, who has a deep love and respect for Jesus who became the Christ, my identity must become the heart, the feet, the hands of the Anointed One. My ego and my true Self must be balanced and must give way to living deep within my essence and being one with the Divine.

REFLECTION

Breathe deeply. Go deep inside and speak your own name aloud. What vibration does it give to you? Is it a strong name, a loving name, a meditative name? Did you have to change your name? Was that difficult? Why or why not? Now examine the many roles you have had in your life.

How did each role, position, career, vocation change your identity? Which ones are you proud of and make you joyful? Are there any that you regret and need self-forgiveness? Why? During the changes in your identity, did you draw closer to God or farther away?

SUGGESTION

Spend some time in appreciation for your name given at birth. Appreciate the various roles you have had or are presently playing in your life. Be grateful for the guidance and presence God has been for you as you moved through the journey of life thus far. Be grateful for your own growth knowing how you have connected with the God who loves you so much.

Be grateful for the joys, the struggles, or even the tragedies in your life. Read over the images of Jesus at the beginning of this chapter. How does one or more fit into your situation? Meditate on them and let Jesus help you with your own identity.

WRITING OPTION

What? Write out your entire name on a piece of paper. Next, do a free write (writing whatever comes into your mind) on your name. Some questions you may try to answer are: how did you write your name? Was it in cursive? Print? What do you notice when you write your name and see it written? Do you write your name with long flowing lines, or shorter scribbles? Does your name flow upward on the page, or downward? Who named you? What do you think about when you write your name in regards to its source (a family name?) or history?

So What? How do you feel about your name? Do you like it? Do you wish it were different? Why or how is your name meaningful for you? Do you feel closer to your family if you have a family name? Or would it be meaningful for you to make a clean break from your past and change your name? Do you know the "meaning" of your name? Do some research on it and write about its meaning. Is your name Biblical? Does it have a religious or mystical background? Does this history change your impression of it? Or yourself?

What Now? Words and names are important for identity—the identity and influence we have on others and the identity we assume for ourselves, as we can see in Genesis 2:20 where Adam names God's creatures. Also think about how we name our pets, and sometimes even plants and cars in our lives.

After having meditated, prayed, thought, and written about names and identity, how do you feel about your personal individuality? Write about how you plan to act or think differently if you are not happy with your identity. If you are happy about your individuality, how might you help others

Chapter 4

HARMONY

The Father and I are one. (John 10:30)
The Paraclete, the Holy Spirit
whom the Father will send in my name
will instruct you in everything,
and remind you of all that I told you.
(John 14:26)

As Christians and as Catholics, we believe in the Trinity. This belief for me is very difficult to wrap my mind around, as it is perhaps for most Christians. It is relatively easy for us to identify with Jesus since He was human, though his miracles, teachings, and His very life were so different from ours. We all have a father, so as Jesus speaks of the Father, we can identify to some extent.

The understanding of the Holy Spirit is another matter. Some people believe, as I do, that the Holy Spirit is the feminine aspect of

God. I have read this in several Spiritual books, and many people I know think of God as Father/Mother, Divine Power/Divine Love, and all that that entails. When I address God, I use Father, Mother, One. God is as much love and nurturing as God is power and wisdom and all the other attributes that we give to God. However, I can easily understand the Holy Spirit as breath, life, one who will instruct us in all things as John says in His gospel. In Matthew 3:16, the image is given to us as a dove. In verse 17, a voice from the heavens says, "This is my beloved Son. My favor rests on Him." In Acts 2:3-4, the Holy Spirit appeared as "Tongues as of fire, and all were filled with the Holy Spirit." From then on, those who were followers of "The Way," as the early Christians were known, were to be baptized with the Holy Spirit.

The concept of Trinity is the image I believe fits the title of this chapter. Trinity speaks of relationship. The Trinity, then, is that three in one, that deep connection existing among Creator, Son, and Spirit, that total working together in deep love.

Most people think of this mystery as a "numbers puzzle." St. Patrick tried to explain Trinity to the Irish using the three-leaf clover —three leaves, one stem. In actuality, the Trinity is not a "numbers" mystery. As we expand upon it, the Trinity is a deep mystical community relationship among the Creator/Artist, Father/Mother, Son/Daughter, Spirit/Motivator, Life/Love. It is through this example of relationship that we ought to live our lives as humanity—humans who are created in the image of God. Therefore, we are born into this mystery of a trinitarian relationship.

It is interesting to me as I remember the six parishes in which I served over the years, three of them were named Holy Trinity—Winsted, Minnesota, Protivin, Iowa, and Des Moines, Iowa.

The image of a team working in harmony has always been important to me, and I have been fortunate to be part of several harmonious teams as I moved through the various ministries in my life.

As I set the stage for one of the most important teams of which I was a part, I remember the story of the time when I injured my back in my early twenties.

I was very young, and we were moving into a new convent. Moving is always back-breaking, and as we moved furniture, refurbished others, carried boxes, and did all that needed to be done to move, I, being strong and young, eager and excited to do my part, ruined my back.

In those days, as I mentioned in the previous chapter, there was no MRI, and X-rays did not find the problem. I spent many years struggling with back pain. Even though I was in pain and sometimes excruciating pain, I continued to teach and tried to live with it as best I could. The large Community with whom I was living was kind and willing to help me, but doctors could not find the problem in my back. To get me more relief from a specialist, I was assigned to a large school in Milwaukee to teach eighth grade. The doctor there prescribed a large heavy back brace, which was somewhat helpful, but not fun to wear. However, after a few years, the pain returned worse than ever.

I experienced a "Trinity" three years later, when I was assigned to Holy Trinity Parish in Protivin, a small Iowa town. There, in a much smaller community, I lived with eight other Sisters, who were "Trinity" to me. Their kindness was outstanding. Sister Connie Brinkoetter, the Superior and principal, led the way. She, who was never ill in her life, understood my pain and my needs in a way no one else had. She, the other Sisters, together with the two priests, who felt part of our Community, took over my class when days were bad, performed many of my other duties, encouraged rest, and spent time with me when I could not be present with the entire group.

My chiropractor helped for a while, but then realized that he could no longer control my pain. He sent me to an excellent osteopathic surgeon in Mason City, Iowa. Connie was my champion, who, together with my parents, helped me through the many and difficult experiences of surgery and recovery. Finally, there was relief after ten years of extreme suffering.

Throughout the rest of my life, however, back trouble has not been far away. It always seems to leave the back burner and move up front. Many times in my life, I have meditated on the meaning of this experience and how I can grow spiritually because of it. There does not seem to be an answer as to WHY, and it has not been easy, but I have always been surrounded with people who care and support. For this I am grateful.

Another "Trinity" experience for me was working in Holy Trinity Parish in Des Moines, Iowa. Seven of us were part of a team. We each were responsible for our own area of ministry: school principal, youth and young adults, director of religious education, adult religious education, visitor to the sick, home-bound and bereaved and the two priests who were responsible for marriage and social justice. However, we all felt a part of the whole.

Each week, we met for lunch, an hour of creative prayer and 2½ hours of sharing. There was kindness, courtesy, and support for each other. But there was also prayer, laughter, fun, and freedom to do the work in our areas. We discussed difficult situations that arose, and the problem was solved without hurting any feelings. We all felt the love and care of each other on the Team. My experience of Holy Trinity Parish in Des Moines was the friendliest (every parishioner and staff including the priests were on a first name basis) and the most wholesome parish I ever knew. Because of that spirit among us, the Staff, the work accomplished in Holy Trinity Parish was phenomenal.

A third experience of "Trinity" was in the Diocese of Des Moines, working with two married men. Being the only woman and the oldest of the three, my thought was that I would be a "fifth wheel on the wagon." Never did I have reason to feel that way. Bill Miller and Ed Kaukman included me in every activity, and respected my gifts and suggestions in each area of our ministry.

Together, we led educational and "getting to know you" meetings and offered retreats for our catechists throughout the diocese. We conducted various kinds of workshops and sacramental Instructions for the parishes and spent time on constructive meetings among ourselves. We attended conferences and did all the tasks needed to introduce and further instruct this small diocese in Southwestern Iowa in the new teachings of Vatican II.

Ed's motto was, "Always live with an 'Attitude of Gratitude'." So in the midst of all our diocesan work, our small team tried to live that motto. Within that context, we found time to pray, laugh, and have fun together. By creating a wonderful team on the diocesan level, our hope was to inspire and exemplify for the parishes we served, to do the same.

Shortly after Vatican II, I had obtained two Master's degrees—in Religious Education and in Sacred Theology. These two invaluable degrees prepared me for the work which we were called upon to do in the Diocese of Des Moines, which was to update catechists and laity in the Documents of Vatican II. Gratefully, we had the support of Bishop Maurice Dingman, who willingly helped Pope John XXIII "throw open the windows of the Church."

The five years I spent in the Des Moines diocese were happy and growth-filled. The years after Vatican II were sacred days for the Church and I, for one, was grateful to have had such an intricate part to play as a Religious Educator in a diocese. I believe that I was able help to make a difference in the religious and spiritual lives of many catechists and laity.

Those "Trinity" experiences, together with a few others I was graced to have over the years, enhanced my spiritual growth and taught me to trust God's constant care, support, and love.

What makes a good team? What are some tools we can apply to live and work in harmony with ourselves and others?

I learned that when I worked with healthy teams, trust, respect, and support for one another were key factors. Today, I also believe that each person needs to take per-sonal responsibility in keeping a healthy balance of body, mind, and spirit. A wise friend once told me that when the body or the mind or the spirit is out of balance, the other two will also be out of balance as well.

Our need is to balance our bodies, as we stay as healthy as possible by eating well, ex-ercising, and being stewards over our physi-cal health, whatever it is that God has given us. We keep our mind balanced by thinking positive thoughts and having a positive attitude. By living as positive and joyful people, we will naturally acquire an attitude of gratitude. And certainly as people who search for God's presence in our lives, it is important to meditate, pray, contemplate, and connect with that Presence. Often we think of prayer only as petition. Our need is also to worship, to honor, and to appreciate the gifts God has given us.

I would like to share two more tools that I found to be very helpful as I check into what makes a healthy team. They are the Enneagram and the Chakra System.

The Enneagram

Many years ago, I began seeing a Spiritual Director who was blind. In the second session, he began telling me about my behavior. This really shocked me. I asked, "How do you know that?"

"It takes one to know one," he responded. "You're an eight."

"What's an eight?" I quickly retorted. He began to explain the Enneagram to me, of which I had never heard.

I now find it to be my favorite tool to understand personalities, and the behavior and integrity of the people with whom I work. Since then I have read several Enneagram books, attended workshops, and taught the system many times to many different groups and individuals. I have used it in my counseling and for my own growth to know better why I behave the way I do and what motivates me in my daily life. Because of the Enneagram, I have become much more non-judgmental and accepting of those around me.

As I become more aware of my own behavior and motivation for the things I do, I find myself thinking, "Oh, that for sure is my 'eight' coming through." An eight is strong, a leader, a protector, a provider, and yes, a maverick. Because of my personality type, I have often "Stuck my foot into my mouth," "stepped on another's toes," showed strong anger, and had to apologize often. BUT I have also stepped out, taken risks, started difficult projects, and with strong energy, has been able to keep several projects going at one time.

My strong energy came through one time when I walked into a room and the person exclaimed, "When you walk in here, your energy fills the whole room." He did not mean it as a compliment. He seemed threatened. As a protector, however, it is easy for an eight to cuddle animals, little children, those who are less fortunate and "the underdog." And I was a great grief counselor!

This chapter gives me an opportunity to share a little understanding of the Enneagram and what it is. However, the Enneagram is a very serious and intensive system, which can be challenging and yet most helpful to the growth of any individual who studies it.

The Enneagram is an ancient tool used over the centuries from teacher to student to help the student grow emotionally and spiritually. The word "Enneagram" comes from the Greek word that means "nine points." Its symbol goes back thousands of years. The modern understanding of the Enneagram began at least in the fourth century. It uses the numbers from one to nine to identify the various personalities. Three numbers emphasize the head—the thinking triad, three emphasize the heart—the feeling triad, and three emphasize the gut—the instinctive triad. Each of the nine types is in us, but we all have our basic type, which does not change. No number or type is better than another. Each can be healthy or unhealthy but when a person knows his or her number, it can be used to understand behavior and motivation, as well as a means for spiritual and psychological growth. The Enneagram helps one note when one is healthy or unhealthy in one's behavior.

Because the Enneagram is built upon numbers, it may be construed as being rigid. It is not at all. When one studies it deeply, there is so much to understand, such as the numbers "winging" into the one next to it, the arrows and subtypes, and suggestions for growth emotionally and spiritually.

There have been many books published on the Enneagram, and new ones continue to come out. Some are presented as a general understanding, some are more geared to the psychological, and some instruct the reader how to grow more spiritually. There are books that work with teams and businesses and books for individual development. There are DVDS and other visual programs as well. Each year, there is an international conference held in cities around the country and chapters around the world. I have attended several of them and found them very useful.

The book I find most helpful for me, which I call my "Bible," is: *The Wisdom of the Enneagram: The Complete Guide to Psychological and Spiritual Growth for the Nine Personality Types*, by Don Richard Riso and Russ Hudson. This book was published in 1999 by Bantam Books and is one of the older publications on the Enneagram. However, it has a wealth of material in its contents. (I spent a week with Don and Russ as they were writing the book and used us for input.)

The Enneagram is really worth looking into for those not familiar with it.

There is much to learn about the Enneagram, but when I begin to teach it, I speak of each number as a reflection of God. The perfection of the ONE, for example, reflects the perfection of God. The nourishing TWO reminds us how God continues to nurture us. The motivation of the THREE makes us aware that God is always urging, begging, pleading, and calling us to connect with God on a deeper level.

As I look at the FOUR, I see the artist, the creator, the Source of this Universe. The innovator FIVE is encouraged to use his God-given ability for research and the improvement of technology, engineering, and through new ways of doing things.

SIXES reflect God in their loyalty, their guardianship and their subtle humor. The adventurist SEVEN teaches the rest of us to imitate God in joy, fun, and freedom. The EIGHT shows us God as the protector, the provider, the leader, the solid rock challenging us to rely totally on God.

And finally, the NINE presents God to us as the healer, the reconciler, comforter, the one who accepts us as we are.

The Chakras

I was introduced to another way of working with inward harmony. Several years ago, I came to understand the chakra system as a means of harmonizing myself from within. The chakras are the energy centers within the body that supply the needed energy to each part. This system comes from the East and was brought over to the West as we began to learn about the value of yoga.

The seven main chakras are aligned along the spine and coincide with the colors of the rainbow. The root chakra is red and is located in the base of the spine. It supplies the energy needed to the lower legs, and feet.

The sacral chakra is orange and builds upon the root chakra, supplying needed energy to the sexual parts of the body.

The yellow third chakra is called the solar plexus chakra and is located between the ribs and belly button. It supplies the energy needed to all those wonderful organs that take care of digestion, purifying the system, elimination, and all the various needs to keep that part of the system healthy.

The heart chakra, which is green, has its own specialty—to supply the energy to the physical heart, and lungs, but also nourishes the loving part of us.

Communication is very important in relationships and in keeping us in harmony with others, so the blue throat chakra has that as its purpose.

As we move up into the head, we are told about the "third eye" chakra, located a little above the eyes in the middle of the forehead. Its color is indigo. This particular chakra supplies energy to the brain, allowing the mind to be active and positive. It opens us up to the higher spiritual realms that surround us. When the third eye is highly developed, it allows some to see, hear, feel, and intuit beyond the ordinary.

And finally, the seventh chakra, the crown chakra, is our connection with the Divine. Its color is purple and is located at the top of our head. It is the source of healing energy, which we need to open so that we can live a life of love, spirituality and healing.

As with the Enneagram, I have also taught the Chakra System several times.

Each time, I personally learn more about it and use the wisdom of each system for my own growth.

It is easy to meditate with the chakras, which helps clear anything negative within us.

One way to clear the chakras is to imagine where they are in each part of the body and to watch the color become brighter and brighter as one imagines them spinning in a spiral clockwise direction.

I have worked with my "third eye," the brow chakra, intensely. This is the chakra that governs the pituitary and pineal glands, giving us the ability to "see," "hear," or intuit beyond our physical senses.

When I retired, I inherited an apartment that had been used by one of our Sisters, Sister Dolores. I had known her well before she died. One night, I could not sleep and went into the kitchen to get a glass of warm milk. Just as I came in, I saw her standing by the cupboard. Because I had known her while she was alive, I was sure it was Sister Dolores; her form was the same as it was when she lived. It was just a few seconds before she was gone. As noted in other places in this book, I have had the privilege of hearing ("clairaudience," as well as seeing ("clairvoyance"). Does that happen because of clearing my chakras? I think so. As with the Enneagram, the chakras have given me an opportunity to find more harmony among my body, mind, emotions and spirit.

Again, I just touched into the tip of what the chakras are and how the knowledge of them can enhance our understanding and our connection with God and others. We can balance and harmonize ourselves within by periodically clearing them and being aware of their purpose. As with the Enneagram, there is much material available, and I encourage the reader to learn more about them through reading, workshops and tapes. By using this information, we can enhance our spiritual, as well as our physical lives.

REFLECTION

Put on some quiet, relaxing music, breathe deeply and close your eyes until any stress you feel leaves you. Check out the groups with whom you worked or are working. Was it or is it really a team? What made it so, or what made it difficult? Examine the reasons if you can. Was there respect, support, non-judgment? If you are involved with a team now, is there something you can do to help the situation?

Has any of them ever learned about the Enneagram or the Chakra system? Would you feel comfortable suggesting that you all learn together? In order for you to feel more a part of a group or a team, do you have to find another job or ministry, or career?

SUGGESTION

If you were on a team who was difficult, spend some time forgiving yourself in any way you may have been part of the problem. If you are ready, but not before, forgive the others so that you can find peace within yourself.

Spend sometime clearing your chakras. Do this by imaging each chakra as you move up the spine. As you do this, see its color and in your imagination watch the color become brighter and more and more beautiful. Notice that each one spins, as we are told that they do. And when you can visualize it spinning in a bright color, go on to the next one, until all of them are bright and cleared.

WRITING OPTION

What? Write the word "personality" on a piece of paper. What is your personality like? In your world, does everything have to be perfect? Do you try to make others perfect, or do you let people be? Do you feel called to be a moralist—black and white, right or wrong, and no in between? Is your specialty teaching or organizing? Why?

Are you the nurturer? The lover? Are you a people pleaser trying to help everyone in your circle, yet do not take care of yourself? Do you consider yourself a good role model? Is image important to you? Do you seek the "Peter Principle," always working to get to the top?

Are you the romantic, the artist? Do your moods take over your behavior? Are you melancholic so that others do not know how you are on any given day? Is your life lived in your head and not in relationships? Do you observe long and hard before joining in? In your mind, are you the expert?

How loyal are you? Are you the traditionalist or open to other thinking? Do you spend time doubting yourself and others and even God? Are you the adventurist, the fun loving person, the planner who never finishes the plans?

Are you strong, harsh, gentle with the down trodden? Do you consider yourself a leader? Do you challenge others just by being who you are?

Are you the peacemaker, the healer? Do you try to reconcile, comfort? Do you merge with society or are you stubborn? Do you feel that you are lazy? What other personality traits do you have not mentioned above?

So What? Think about several aspects of your personality. List them. Which aspects delight you? Which ones embarrass or sadden you? Why? Are there some aspects of your personality you wish to change? Which ones? Do you know how to go about changing some part of your personality? In general, do you really like yourself? Why? Why not? Do you feel you have a healthy self -esteem? If not, what keeps you stuck? Now write about why these things are meaningful for you. Why are they so important?

What Now? Relationships are imperative to make friends, lead others and to work and live in harmony with those around you. An important part of this is to consciously develop a deep and true love of self— learning to honor your own personality because of your integrity and spiritual growth.

Jesus said, "Love your neighbor AS YOURSELF." After listing various traits of your personality, spend some quality time expressing gratitude for the work you have already accomplished in your growth in holiness and in relationships.

Check into other tools, such as the Enneagram and Chakras, to learn new ideas for dealing harmoniously with others. For this exercise, write about what you are going to do to express your gratitude to those in your life who have had a positive impact on you. Take action: write down the address of the nearest library and its phone number so you can call to see if they have books on the Enneagram or Chakras if you feel moved to use those systems. Or just write about how you might work in more harmony with yourself and others.

Chapter 5

LOVE

Love has no room for fear;
rather, perfect love casts out all fear.
And since fear has to do with punishment,
Love is not yet perfect in one who is afraid.
We, for our part,
love because He first loved us.
(1John 4:18-19)

What is love really?

The word *love* is one of those nebulous words and ideas that have been grossly overused and misunderstood in our society. It is bounced around from, "I love spaghetti and meatballs," to, "I have a deep love for my spouse," to, "I love God with all my heart." Love seems to have as many connotations and as many meanings as there are people who talk about it. Because of this, I struggled to write about love, but was encouraged to do so by friends and others who knew about my writing. Perhaps my ideas and experiences will give you a new understanding of love, which may benefit your life.

The word itself—and every attempted meaning of love—is explored in millions of books, magazines, movies, television, computers, and every other media available to people. Each person has his or her own take on what love means. I do, too. I have loved many persons and things. But as I reflect over my many years, I realize that my love for friends, family, special persons, varied ministries, pets, things, and places I have been in my life were only degrees of a greater Love. Each manifestation of love was in some way important, for it led me to finding the most important LOVE of my life. That love is the love I have for God and the love God has for me. Other loves are only a flavor, a taste, a hint, which bring on a yearning for the merging of my heart with the Heart of Christ.

One of the fathers and doctors of the Catholic Church, St. Augustine of Hippo, even wrote in his *Confessions*, "Our hearts are restless until they rest in Thee, O God."

As I move through this chapter, and express my understanding of love in my life, I would hope that you would find the importance of understanding the meaning of love in your life and in the end realize that you, too, are called to be a mystic.

How did I learn how to love? I certainly felt it from my parents and siblings and I felt it in a very different way from those wonderful horses on the farm. And as I grew in various friendships, I felt love and shared it with many persons in my life both in and out of my School Sisters of St. Francis Community.

Then, at one time in my younger life, I felt a different and new kind of love. A man came into my life. We worked together, and I received much of his attention until we realized we were "in love." There was no sex, but there was a deep love and caring for each other. Guilt was there, but after we were no longer working together and the depth of love subsided, I spent much time reflecting on what that period in my life meant for my spiritual life. Slowly I began to realize that the love I had felt for him taught me the meaning of human love as I had not experienced it before. His love was a different kind of love from the love I had received from my parents or friends, and of course, my beloved horses. My work now was to learn to transfer that love to Jesus in a way I had not known how to do before.

Some in our society think of love only in terms of sex. Others question what it means for them. Because love is truly a mystery, lifetimes are spent trying to understand it and solve its mystery. Perhaps to understand and to live a life of love are the most difficult jobs each of us will ever do in our lifetime.

I had a counselee many years ago who, after several years of marriage and finally a divorce, was struggling with the whole concept of real love. I asked this young woman if she had ever really been in love with her husband. She had married very young, and I wondered whether she understood what "being in love" meant for her.

Her response, "I think I was in love with love." A very interesting answer and perhaps one that is more universal than is believed! Being in love with love! Perhaps that is the understanding that some people have as they talk about love.

Everyone seeks love, for it is our food, our nourishment, and our very life. Love opens our world to wider consciousness. When we are in love and loving, we change our attitudes, our behaviors, and our reasons for living. When love is lacking, our lives become totally bereft of goodness and joy. Rather, they become sterile and rigid. Often that is followed by bitterness, anger, critical behavior, and even cruelty. Because so many individuals in our society lack love to such a great extent, I believe society itself has become dysfunctional.

In my life, I realize that human love is a direct realization of God's love for me. Many years ago, I took a theology course on the German Jesuit theologian, Karl Rahner. I struggled through the course, because Karl Rahner was very difficult to read and to understand. However, from his theology, I learned that God is always inviting, pleading, begging, and gracing us to love Him/Her. And our response to that grace is also God's gift. Rahner's message was difficult for me to comprehend for a long time. Do I not have free will? Where is my part in that invitation?

Is my love in any form only found in the love God has for me? I finally came to the conclusion that if God is first in my life, I become involved with the consciousness of God and/or Christ. Any good and holy action on my part becomes God's good and holy action. God, then, uses us for the good of others as well as ourselves. Maybe that is what Karl Rahner meant; maybe it was not. The understanding has served me well to keep in touch with the love God bestows on me each day.

Perhaps a few words about this very prolific German author might help here. Karl Rahner was one of seven theologians invited by Pope John XXIII, the originator of Vatican II, to develop the document, *Lumen Gentium,* which is a dogmatic explanation of the doctrine of the church. In 1976, *The Foundation of Christian Faith* was published and encompassed many of his lectures and essays on numerous topics of Christianity. *The Encyclopedia of Theology,* written toward the end of his life (1984) is another book including many Christian topics. The main idea of Rahner's theology was: All human beings have a latent experience of God in any perception of meaning or "transcendental experience."

When I was a college student many years ago, a story circulated among another group of college students about a woman who was their professor. She was quite small and elderly. When the students entered the classroom on the first day, she hugged each one of them. Laughter broke out among some of the students who were not in her class.

"Did you get a hug from her every day, " one asked?

"No," was the reply, "but she hugged us with her eyes." That little woman was truly a gift of love to her students. Her gaze gave each one of them her own self, her own gift of love each day as the students entered her classroom. Because of this teacher's "hugs," I am sure that her students became better people and perhaps also better students.

I try to remember that story when I look into the face of a child, at a sick or elderly person struggling with life, persons who are in deep grief, friends or family very dear to me, and even animals and the beautiful world around us. I make the effort to hug them with my eyes, thereby sending my own gift of love out into the universe. Sometimes, I succeed.

As I struggled in my younger life to know a greater love for Jesus, He would not be out-done in generosity. Jesus showed real love for me with a wonderful experience many years later. I realized then that God is not bound by rules. The revelation of God can manifest itself at any time and in any place and to any person that God chooses to do so. This perception of God's love is guided by Karl Rahner's theology.

One day, while I lived in Santa Fe, I was invited to participate in a retreat that was based on divine principles and the higher states of consciousness. The retreat, con-ducted by a woman and her daughter, consisted of guided meditations, discussion, and some instruction. One afternoon, as the director guided us through a meditation us-ing the twelve dimensions of consciousness (explained below), I became very centered as I moved deeper and deeper into meditation.

By the time the director reached the twelfth dimension and guided us through some of the tenets of that dimension, which is a deep connection with God, I felt that I was in touch with my entire being in a way I had never been before, and I felt one with all that is.

Suddenly, I felt and saw the Heart of Jesus descend from above me and come down to merge with my heart. His heart totally enveloped mine so that my heart was within His. As the heart, which was detached from a body, slowly moved towards my heart, it enveloped it and became one with mine. As His heart slowly descended, the color of the heart and the surrounding area was red and sparkling.

What a gift! I was overwhelmed! I had never felt such a deep love of Jesus before. Feelings of awe and exhilaration took over. That image continues to nourish me when life becomes stressful and difficult. My devotion to the Heart of Jesus has taken on new meaning, one that puts me into a space of deep connection with Jesus' Heart. That experience made me realize that God is not inhibited in any way by our humanity, but wills freely to extend love and grace to me or to anyone else whom God chooses.

There are many pictures in the Catholic world of the Sacred Heart. Most of them present Jesus with His heart exposed outside the body, but with a picture of Him behind it. What I saw was something different. I saw only the heart—no face, no body. Just the heart alone and it was very beautiful.

As I pray to the Sacred Heart, I find it more satisfying to spend time being caressed by Him, which seems more appropriate for me as I continue my devotion to the Heart of Jesus. For example, a few years ago, I was in a small chapel dedicated to the Sacred Heart. This beautiful little chapel contained a marble statue of Jesus holding a person on His lap. There was no heart exposed. It was very lovely and very fitting.

There is much material about the Twelve Dimensions on the Internet. For more information, I encourage that you to check out *The 12 Dimensions of Creation, Parts I, II, and III*, by Owen Waters. He also has material on the Internet called, *Dimensions of Consciousness* and an essay called *The Conscious Universe*. This material will give the reader a deeper understanding than I am able to provide within the scope of this book.

What do I understand by the Twelve Dimensions? Owen Waters states that a dimension is a state of consciousness and a means of organizing different plans of existence. The Twelve Dimensions are also called the Multiple Dimensions of Existence, which teach that there are multiple movements towards God. The Twelve Dimensions provide a concrete context, which can contain all dimensions of the Universe, and which the scientific community also supports. Understanding the Twelve Dimensions helps me in my search for God and for love. The tenet of understanding the Twelfth Dimension is:

> *The Point where all consciousness knows*
> *itself as one with All That Is i.e., God*
> *Where there is no separation*
> *between the created and the Creator*
> *Where one knows that we are one*
> *with the Creator.*
> *When one knows without a doubt*
> *that he/she is a spark of God,*
> *that person will never be the same.*

As I understand consciousness, I think of it as the Buddha calls it—*being awake*—awareness of "Who We Are" in our connection with God. It is an awareness of being in touch with the reality beyond ourselves. This comes out of a place where we realize that there is no separation between God and myself. Consciousness is that recognition that we and our Creator are one, that we are a spark of God, a wave in the ocean of God's love. When we gets to that point, there is no turning back. The love of God takes over. That is the mind and Heart of Jesus.

God can and will show infinite presence in any place and to anyone whom S/He desires to reveal the gift of love. It is God's choice and not ours. We are merely recipients of the gift. All we need to do is to honor it and fall in love all over again.

I believe that is what St. Therese of Lisieux, St. John of the Cross, and all those wonderful mystics experienced as they sought and lived in union with God.

I know I am far from that wonderful experience, but it is something that I, and all humans, can strive for since our heritage is to be one with our Creator—that spark in which we really KNOW that we are made in the image and likeness of God.

As humans, we are still individuals with our own personality, our own desires, and our own individuality. However, when we allow ourselves to consciously surrender, the ego is balanced with the soul and holiness can grow. That God energy can transcend our own limitations.

My devotion to the Heart of Jesus has, for me, been a way of re-directing the God-Self. Even though I have a long way to go, I recognize that I must keep myself centered and strive to become totally absorbed in the beloved, and to no longer be separate. Often, my prayer becomes a petition to join with the Sacred Heart and to extend His Light and blessings to those around us and into the whole world. For me, that Beloved is Jesus, and I am an expression of His love. I like to keep a picture of the Heart of Jesus near me as a reminder of that special day. It also reminds me that I have a need for transformation, for constant conversion, and for constant surrender.

Was my experience of the Heart of Jesus imagination? I think not! Is imagination real? It certainly is as real as thinking or feeling, ideas or memories. Can we grow through imagination? I believe using our imagination through meditation can be a source of growth. It has been for me.

I do not know for certain if Jesus was really present that afternoon. I believe that He was. I know what I saw and what I felt. I do know, however, that the experience made a deep impression on me. It gave me a greater hunger for prayer, and created a dynamic shift within my being. The experience lasted only a few moments. Although, I cannot continuously live in that experience, the fruit of it has enhanced my life. Perhaps that was the only purpose of the meditation and of the entire retreat. That was my experience and my devotion. Each person will be invited into his/her own way to holiness.

Nurturing the imagination is another way that God invites, pleads, begs, and graces us. We nurture our imagination the same way that we nurture our thinking process, i.e., by stimulation and practice. The more we do that, the more creative we become, and hence the more we reach into ourselves and learn about our motivations and behavior patterns.

One of the School Sisters of Saint Francis, who taught high maintenance second grade children in a public school, told me how she tried to help the children to grow and form better behavior patterns. She told me that when she had a child who was especially naughty that day, she would go home and in her imagination, take that child into her arms, rock him and tell him that she loves him, and explain to him why he should change his behavior. She told me how much it helped and often the child would psychically get her message. This is surely a very creative way to extend love to a child and to develop imagination.

Many years ago, I was making a directed Jesuit retreat. As my meditation for the day, I was directed to read the first letter of John. That was a very familiar and loved passage, which I had read many times before, but I never really "got it." Sometimes, we read something many times and do not get it. That day was different. As I read the passage, the words shouted out to me. My understanding and belief that love and hate were opposite were changed forever. John says, "Love casts out fear," and "love has no room for fear" (1 John 4:18). For the first time, I became aware that love and fear are opposites, not love and hate. This was a real revelation for me.

As I spent some time thinking about what fear does to me and others, I recognize that fear paralyzes. Fear is one of those energies that hold us back from connecting with ourselves, with others, and with God. When I hold onto fear, I find that I am in a constant state of distraction over what I worry or am fearful about. Fear, of course, is an emotion that can save us from danger, and it, at times, is a saving grace, but living in deep fear keeps us from loving.

Psychiatrists tell us that underneath our ordinary fears, is the fear of death, fear for our own survival. From my experience of working in the funeral home, I found that to be true. Even for those who could see peace on the face of their loved one as the person died, it did not erase the fear the survivor experienced, nor the fear the departed had before peace had settled in—fear of the unknown, fear of suffering, fear of leaving loved ones behind, fear of not going to heaven, fear of still having unfinished business, and many other fears that take over the mind at such a time.

What would it be like for us to transcend that fear? In order to do that, we must begin to look beyond the body-mind. We must, "Put on the mind of Christ, (1 Corinthians 2:16) and live the words of Scripture, "I no longer live, but Christ lives in me" (Galatians 2:20). More important, however, we must not only invite Christ to live within, but we who seek to be relieved from fear, must live as Christ!

One day, when talking about the spiritual life with someone, that person said, "We need to stop following Christ. Rather, we must be Him." This is so true, but so difficult.

One other point needs to be included in this chapter. Jesus said, "Love your neighbor as yourself" (Mark 12:31). I really do not think that most people, whether they are religious or not, understand what that message from Jesus really means. For me, loving

SELF really means freedom from fear, freedom from judgment, freedom from hatred, freedom from revenge and as nations, freedom from war. Loving self would keep us from thinking in terms of "we and they," and "us and them."

Paraphrasing St. Paul in 1 Corinthians 13:4-8, which is very often read for weddings and at Mass, Paul says, "Love is patient, kind, not jealous, does not put on airs, snobbish, never rude, self seeking, not prone to anger, does not rejoice in the wrong, but rejoices in the truth. There is no limit to love's forbearance, its trust, its hope, its power to endure. Love never fails." This, for me, is what loving ourselves and others really means—connecting with self and others through our soul. Most of the time, we love others because they are friends, or good to us, or belong to the same class or group or tribe. We judge others because they are poor, or black, or gay, or Muslim, or "beneath us," or slow, or crabby, or dozens of other reasons. That is when we "love" through our ego.

What do I mean by this? If we connect with others through our ego or personality, we look at others and judge them. If we could look at others as ourselves, both we, and they are made in God's image, then our thoughts would be kinder. If we could live our lives in the wisdom that "all are created equal," barriers would be broken down, and the thinking of those who are "different" from us would be meaningless. Love would truly cast out fear!

REFLECTION

Bring yourself into a peaceful sensation through your breath and deal with any stress or burdens within your body by releasing them. Then place yourself into a space of imagination and remembrance.

What does love mean to you? How did you learn to love? Who in your life gives you inspiration and teaches you the gift of wisdom? What good or difficult experiences have you had with love? Are there experiences in your life that cause you to feel guilty around this thing called "love?"

Spend some time recognizing the fear patterns in your life. How can you transform them into love? Do they have to do with death? Do you really love yourself? Where do God and/or Christ fit into your life?

SUGGESTION

Just sit for a few minutes and observe your life of love. Be grateful for however love was brought into your being, whether it was in childhood or your adult life.

If there is guilt for any reason, face the reality and forgive yourself. If you feel love is lacking and you feel bitter or angry, it may be time to find a way to let go and bring some change into your life.

If you feel inspired to spend some time with a friend or spiritual mentor and to share this mysterious aspect of yourself, bring all to prayer and be willing to give yourself that gift.

WRITING OPTION

What? Write about one time when love made a real difference in your life. This love does not have to be a romantic love; it might be the love you felt for a parent or mentor. It might be the love you felt from someone else. Or it might be a love that you witnessed between two other people, for example, the love you noticed when a nurse or teacher spent extra time with someone in their care. It might even be an especially moving story from the Bible or another religious or spiritual text that told a story involving love.

So What? How did this experience of love make you feel? How did it change your life or how you loved yourself or someone else? Why was this loving experience meaningful for you?

What Now? Write about how you plan to spread the love you witnessed and experienced to others. If you've experienced self-doubt or fear in your life, you might also write about how you plan to use love to help you heal these wounds and move through them to reach a more loving state.

Chapter 6

WORTHINESS

This is what Yahweh asks of you:
To Act justly,
To Love tenderly and
To Walk humbly with your God
(Micah 6:8)

"Relax, Arlene, relax; just relax!" Those were the only words I said to myself in 1983, as I floated on my back in the Atlantic Ocean. I had been invited by Mary Ann, a Sister friend, to enjoy a week with her and another Sister in Florida at Mary Ann's family cottage by the ocean.

All week, the three of us had a wonderful time playing in the water. It was now July 4th and time for one more fun-time at noon the day before going home. Only Mary Ann and I went to the ocean that day, and I, who do not swim but knew how to float on my back, always held onto someone's hand. That day, it was Mary Ann's.

Suddenly, we were separated. I was up to my neck in water and yelled, "I can't get out of here."

Mary Ann yelled back, "Float to me." There was nothing for me to do, but get onto my back, but I floated farther and farther away from shore. Unknown to me, I was in a rip tide.

Mary Ann dashed out of the water and yelled, "There's a woman out there drowning." Two lifeguards, who "happened" to be walking the private beach, immediately went into action, swimming as fast as possible toward me. Two others joined, and as I kept on floating out and out and telling myself to relax, they finally reached me and struggled to get me back to shore. After they checked to make sure my lungs were not filled with water, and that I was basically OK, they left. Four young people I had never met saved my life and I did not even learn their names!

It was perhaps the most harrowing experience I had ever had. I was thoroughly shaken for days to come and even now the memory is very real and disturbing.

As I reflected on this event over the years, several thoughts came to me. I did not pray. I did not think. I now know that if I would have, I would have gone down. I can only believe that the angels or some others in the Spirit World held me above water. Three years later during a directed retreat, I recalled the experience and my body felt an overwhelming gratitude. What else could I do except to offer a prayer for them and plead that they were grace-filled wherever they may be.

I called this chapter, "Worthiness." Why was I worthy to be rescued? What makes me or anyone worthy? Some will say that there was more for me to do in this lifetime. I question that, especially when children and babies are being buried every day. Perhaps another way of thinking about worthiness is to recognize that we really are worthy, not for what we do, but for what God, our Creator, has done for us. As often mentioned, we are made in the image and likeness of God. That means we are part of who God is—one with our Source Energy. In addition, we, as Christians, have been baptized, i.e., invited into a

Community of others who are also made in God's image. Other religions have their own rites, or ceremonies that invite their future members into their communities who are also made in God's image. And even those who profess to belong to no community of faith, or even do not believe in God, have still been made in God's image. Are they worthy?

The dictionary notes worthiness as having value, being honorable or important. I see worthiness as akin to spirituality. As an example of the connection of worthiness to spirituality, is a book by Anthony de Mello.

Anthony de Mello, a Jesuit known throughout the world for his writings and spiritual conferences died suddenly in 1987. His book called *Awareness, The Perils and Opportunities of Reality*, published in 1990 and edited by J. Francis Stroud, S.J., after de Mello's death, is filled with delightful anecdotes and stories that give another understanding to the whole meaning of worthiness.

A few of the delightful titles of his stories are: "On Wanting Happiness," "Good, Bad or Lucky," "Finding Yourself," and "Stripping Down to the 'I'." From this book, I learned that we are more than people of flesh and blood. We are not just a physical being having a soul or a spirit; we are spiritual beings in physical bodies with spirits and souls that need to be nourished.

Every religion has various means of nourishing the spirit through ritual, prayer, fasting, and special days. There are many other ways of nourishing the spirit within us: spending time in appreciation of nature, meditation, spiritual reading, listening to inspiring music, reading sacred texts, such as the Bible, the Torah, and the Koran. In doing so, we give ourselves the opportunity to grow spiritually and become more "honorable."

I see growth in spirituality as another way of becoming credible in society. How do I reach out to others? How do I bring Light and spread peace in my own small world, my country, and the world at large? How do I give back to society the gifts and talents I have received, all the while being grateful for them? How do I appreciate my spouse, my children, my friends, my health? In other words, how do I become holier, moving toward the ideal of mysticism—merging with the mind and Heart of Christ—of God?

When Jesus was in the Garden of Gethsemane, He left the Apostles to go a short distance to pray. When He returned, He asked a simple question, "Could you not stay awake for even one hour with me?" (Matthew 26:40). I believe this question had a much deeper meaning. The Apostles were physically asleep, but in truth, they were asleep to the reality of what was going on at the time. Were they not aware that there was something sacred happening, after the experience of breaking bread and witnessing the washing of the feet and Jesus' teachings at the Last Supper?

It seems that most of us are asleep as we go about our lives from our birth to our death. Each day, we go about our work, our relaxation, our entertainment, our daily duties, but we are asleep. We sleep through all the beauty around us, the goodness of our human existence, the reality of living a deeper spiritual life, and the need to nourish our souls. In other words, we miss the opportunity to become more aware, more conscious, and more in touch with the presence of God within.

Spirituality, becoming more "worthy," more "honorable," then, is that constant struggle to wake up to the reality of God's presence in our world and within us.

As a Christian, I would like to reflect on who Jesus is for me and on a few of Jesus' teachings that have helped me in my awakening. Jesus' teachings are really universal and available to all.

In Matthew 16:13-20, we read the story of Jesus asking the disciples the question, "Who do people say that the Son of Man is? "Who is this Jesus, this Rabbi, this 'messiah'?" Jesus was asking about the neighborhood gossip.

"Well," the Disciples answered, "some say John the Baptist, others Elijah, and still others Jeremiah or one of the prophets."

"Who do you say that I am?"

As the rest of the Apostles were wondering what to say, the impetuous Peter answered, "You are the Messiah, the Son of the Living God." Peter was applauded and the Apostles were probably relieved!

Who do I say Jesus is? We all must search for that answer in our own lives. I heard a wonderful homily many years ago on this particular story. I will paraphrase his ending: as the priest finished speaking about the Gospel message, he said, "Jesus is whoever you need Him to be at any time in your life. Sometimes, you may need a friend, at another time, a beloved, another time you may need a counselor, another time a teacher, and still another time a compassionate forgiver. Let Him be whoever you need Him to be at the significant times in your lives."

In the 1970s, when I was studying for my Master's Degree in Religious Education, I took a very informative course, "The Jesus of History and the Christ of Faith." We studied Jesus as He walked upon this earth. We talked about His incarnation and babyhood, as He was nourished and nurtured by His mother. We spoke about our images of Him as a toddler, learning to walk and talk and play. His wonderful mother, Mary, taught Him how to pray, to study the Psalms, to worship in the synagogue, and to do all the things little Jewish boys were expected to do. Mary and Joseph watched Jesus grow into a teenager and worried about Him when He was lost in the Temple. How proud they were of their son as He grew into manhood!

In class, we speculated about what He did and where He went during those adult years before He began His ministry in what we now call the Holy Land. Did He go back to Egypt to study with the ancients in that land? Was He in India as many claim? Did He belong to the Essenes, a mystical group at the time? How did He become the great teacher, the miracle worker, the "Son of God?" Did He know He was God from the beginning of His life, or did He gradually accept that?

We studied His miracles, His teachings, His prophecies, His parables, and His death and Resurrection. Most important, however, was, who is the Christ of Faith? What did Jesus leave His followers? His Ministry had changed everything for those who became His followers and eventually for the entire Christian world.

The class was now invited to understand who Jesus was for us as we moved on in our own spiritual growth.

I began to think through who is the Christ, the Anointed One, the Savior, the Messiah, the Redeemer, and all the other names Jesus has been given. *The human Jesus interpreted God for me.*

I believe that the most important work Jesus had to do while He was on this earth was to tell us, teach us, give examples of who God is—who our Father/Mother God really is! We speak about God as Protector, Almighty, Creator, Artist, Miracle Worker, Pure Being, Eternal, Universal Infinite, and more—trying to understand God as much as humans can attempt to do so. However, we as humans make God in our own image, even though we make the pronouncement that we are made in His/Her image. We make God the angry God, the scary God, the punitive God, the revengeful God, the distant God, the uninterested God, the God we cannot rely on to answer our prayers, the God who deserted us when our health failed, when our child took the wrong path, when our loved one died, when divorce was inevitable, and times when we really needed that God, S/He abandoned us.

How did Jesus interpret His Father, His Mother for us? The vision that Jesus gave us was so new and so radical and so breathtaking that a whole new religion, Christianity, was inspired by that interpretation. Jesus taught by stories, the best way humans learn, and sometimes He taught in obscurity.

Through all the stories and teaching, Jesus identified totally with LOVE, and He is absolute about that. In John 13:35, we read, "By this will all know that you are my disciples, that you love one another." The first Christians learned it well. In the *Acts of the Apostles*, the early Christians were identified by "See how these Christians love one another." If we learn nothing else about Jesus, as He teaches us about God, we must think of God as Love.

Shortly before Jesus died, He gave His last discourse, His dying wish. In John 13:34-35, He says, "I give you a new Commandment: Love one another. Such as my love has been for you, so must your love be for each other. This is how all will know you are my disciples: your love for one another." He was insistent that before He left us, He would make sure that message got through to us humans. Jesus made Love a commandment—He said, a new Commandment I give to you. Love one another as I have loved you!

In Matthew 5:43-44, Jesus also taught us another very important lesson. Jesus says, "You have heard it said, 'You shall love your neighbor and hate your enemy.' My command to you is: love your enemies, pray for your persecutors." And in Matthew 18:21-22, we read, then Peter came up and asked him, "Lord, when my brother wrongs me, how often must I forgive him? Seven times?" "No," Jesus replied, "not seven times; I say to you seventy times seven times."

We also learn, however, that forgiveness was not practiced in those days. Forgiveness was a foreign concept to the thinking of people at the time of Jesus. It was an eye for an eye and a tooth for a tooth. Nevertheless, on the cross, Jesus gave us the example of total forgiveness: "Father forgive them. They do not know what they are doing" (Luke 23:34).

I made some suggestions about love and forgiveness in the previous chapter on love. Here, however, I will give a few more thoughts about my thinking of who Jesus is for me and the reason I am "worthy" to be His follower—to be Him.

"The Kingdom of God is within you." This passage is such a mystery because most of us think of the Kingdom of God as Heaven. Yet Jesus says it is within us. So when we sit silently and perhaps say a prayer, or just ponder His Incarnation, His sufferings, His Sacred Heart, His love of children, His healing the blind, the lame or the suffering humankind, what we are doing is connecting with the Divine. As we contemplate the image of Jesus in any way we like, we recognize His love, His compassion, His kindness, His forgiveness, and His tenderness and care.

Perhaps those images are the inspiration to put some of His wonder into action. That Divine connection is our very essence—who we really are—part of God and all that God wishes us to be. Thus, the Kingdom of God is being formed within us as we learn how to live it.

Jesus also said, "Be in the world but not of it." As is recorded, St. Francis of Assisi is remembered for several beautiful prayers and poetry. One that is universal is: *"Lord, make me an instrument of your peace. Where there is hatred, let me sow love. Where there is injury, pardon. Where there is despair, hope. Where there is darkness, Light, Where there is sadness, joy,"* and so on. Living that prayer is being in the world, but not of it.

Another way is really trying to be the hands and feet, the words and works, the thought and actions of Jesus. St. Teresa of Avila once said:

> *Christ has no body now, but yours.*
> *No hands, no feet on earth, but yours.*
> *Yours are the eyes through which*
> *Christ looks compassion into the world.*
> *Yours are the feet*
> *Through which Christ walks to do good.*
> *Yours are the hands*
> *With which Christ blesses the world.*

I have heard people say, "Oh, that is for priests and nuns." Priests and nuns were not sitting on the hillsides of Galilee, nor were they standing beneath the cross, nor watching Jesus listen with kindness and compassion to those who were hurting. They were the merchants, the farmers, the carpenters, the housewives, the children, the Samaritans, and yes, the Rabbis, and even the tax collectors, the "you and I" who Jesus was teaching. They were the people open enough to believe in Him and recognize who He was—the Messiah, the Son of the Living God. Some Pharisees, and Sadducees, the priests and Levites—the important people of the Temple as well as the civic population were not the listening types. They knew all the answers. They were the criticizers, the gripers, the ones who finally made sure He was killed.

Jesus also said, "My yoke is easy and My burden is light (Matthew 11:30). Most of the time, we don't believe that, especially when life gets more and more difficult. But the closer we get to being God conscious, the easier life becomes.

I have a friend who grew up atheist, but has now accepted God into his life. One day, I asked him what difference that has made. His answer, "Life became a lot easier."

Somehow obstacles are removed and trust becomes a greater part of life.

The best exercise we can do is to "Go with the flow." Surrender! When we resist or try to control and/or have too high of expectations for ourselves or others, life just does not work. The more we hang loose when we meet a situation that causes us anger or frustration, or fear, the more God can take over.

As an "eight" on the Enneagram, I know that to be very hard. The "eight" is very controlling, so I had and still have much work to do. But Jesus said, "I give you my assurance, whatever you ask the Father, He will give you in my name" (John 16:23). Many people do not believe that. Many people have said to me, "I pray and pray and pray, and God does not answer my prayers."

I have a DVD recorded by an actor named Paul Link. He acted in the very old T.V. series called *Chips*. He tells his story of the time that his young wife discovered breast cancer while nursing their second child. She struggled with alternatives and with chemo and tried various cancer centers in the United States and even in Mexico. The couple and their friends and family prayed and prayed for her healing.

Then to their shock, she was pregnant again. The doctor wanted her to have an abortion. I will never forget what Paul reported her saying, "How can I put poison into my body, when I will not even put it into my garden?" The doctor also told her that if she bore that child, she would not live longer than a year. She had a beautiful little girl and lived one year and three days.

As Paul in the DVD reports, she was not healed from cancer, but the miracle was their little Rose. God sometimes answers prayer in ways that is somehow for our highest good and not what we wish for. God does not need our prayers; we need to pray. Prayer brings us to a deeper connection and trust of God.

Perhaps most readers of this book are Catholic Christians or others who hold Christianity as their belief. But even if you are not a practicing Christian, Christ's messages may have meaning and value for your spiritual journey toward God. For Christians, there is the constant invitation and need to ponder Jesus, the human being whose life in many ways mirrors our own with its problems, changes, pain, and joys as He moved through Bethlehem, Nazareth, Galilee, and finally Jerusalem.

He was the wisdom teacher as seen in the Gospels that are rich in parables, stories, symbols and instructions. Through this method, Jesus gave us the inspiration and the knowledge we need to be people of peace, of compassion, of love, and of kindness. He is the miracle worker telling us that we, too, can move mountains if we have faith and He says that we can do greater things than He. Jesus is the true mystic. He was totally merged with the mind and heart of God. And He is Divine: "Everything has been given over to me by my Father. No one knows the Son but the Father and no one knows the Father but the Son—and anyone to whom the Son wishes to reveal him" (Matthew 11:27).

So when and how do we become more worthy? For anyone interested in growth in the spiritual life, to respond to the call to be a mystic, it is helpful to read and meditate on the teachings of Jesus and other sacred writings. It is advantageous to spend time in nature and to enjoy beautiful music and other sources of beauty. Most of all, it is important to deal with our own negative and hurt feelings. These are some of the ways to value ourselves and others more fully. Our prayer then can be one of gratitude: Lord I am worthy because your gifts have made me worthy.

REFLECTION

When do you feel unworthy? Why? Who and what have taught you that you are not worthy? Parents? Teachers? Religion? Society? Bosses? When you say as Catholics, Lord, I am not worthy, what goes through your mind? How do you respond? Can you in truth begin to believe in your own worth? What must you do to recognize your worth?

SUGGESTION

Sit for a time in quiet and enjoy your breath. Name our Mother/Father/God as you connect at this time in your life—Creator, Protector, Nurturer, and so on. Spend some time in worship, praise, and gratitude for the guidance you have received during your lifetime.

If Jesus has been a part of your life, be grateful for that experience. Resolve to make an effort to live an "attitude of gratitude" as you go about your daily tasks. Remind yourself that you are worthy and can become more awake and aware and valuable to yourself and others.

WRITING OPTION

What? Write about a time when you did not feel worthy in some way. Was it at school? At work? Was it with a loved one? At church? What happened? Were you able to move through this? Are you still burdened with these feelings?

So What? Why was this incident meaningful for you? What made this moment of unworthiness so powerful or painful? Why was it so important, or why is it so important, to you now?

What Now? If you were not able to work through that feeling of unworthiness, write about what you plan to do to try to move beyond it. Put into words your action plan for feeling worthy again and your ideas for moving into oneness with God who made you worthy by creating you in His image.

If these precise steps are unclear to you now, perhaps you might write about what you think you need to do to clarify your path. These steps might include speaking with a spiritual advisor or counselor.

Chapter 7

PRESENCE

*Teach them to carry out everything
I have commanded you. And know
That I am with you always,
until the end of the world.*
(Matthew 29:20)

"Arlene, forget Milford, and get your-self to Santa Fe!" These daunting words were loud and clear inside of me at Mass on August 15, 1990.

What could they mean? My first thought was that I could be institutionalized for hear-ing voices! One does not hear voices in Toledo, Ohio! I said nothing to the other four Sisters with whom I was living. Then nine nights later (the length of a novena, such as I had made dozens of times in my life), I had a dream. (Novenas have been prayed for many years by Catholics up to this day. It is a cho-sen prayer that is said each day for nine days usually to a saint for a special favor. Many novenas have been answered and there is a fervent belief in their power.)

In the dream, I was in front of a large mud puddle. I had on Jesuit shoes. What are Jesuit shoes? As in most dreams, one knows things that make no sense in our wake time. Thus, in my dream, I decided to put on Franciscan shoes. I then crossed the mud. I awoke at two o'clock in the morning and contemplated this unusual dream.

"OK," I said to myself, "I am a Franciscan, not a Jesuit. What does the dream mean?" No answer came. When morning dawned, I arose and was able to remember every detail. I began to write down the dream in my journal and again, I heard the distinct voice inside me, "No, Arlene, the city of St. Francis." Before I explain what happened in the city of St. Francis, it is probably helpful if I take a moment to explain some of the key differences between Franciscans and Jesuits.

As mentioned, I am a Franciscan. My religious Community follows the rule of St. Francis of Assisi, who lived from 1182-1226 A.D. His charismatic personality endeared him to many during his lifetime and even to this day. He lived extreme poverty and is especially honored for many facets of his life, among them his love of animals, the environment, and some favorite prayers and songs.

St. Francis also founded a contemplative order of women, known as the Poor Clares. The Poor Clares spend their time in prayer and silence. They do not minister in society. However, out of these two orders founded by St. Francis, many others have arisen, both male and female.

Many books have been written about St. Francis, even a few by his followers while he still lived. A biography which is very readable and interesting is: *The Road to Assisi: The Essential Biography of St. Francis* by Paul Sabatier (Paraclete, 2003).

The Jesuits, also known as the Society of Jesus, is an entirely male order, founded by St. Ignatius of Loyola (1491-1556). Their main ministry has always been in education. Thus, the Jesuits sponsor many colleges, universities, and high schools, as well as ministering in some parishes. A special part of the Jesuit Order is their spirituality known as the Exercises of St. Ignatius, which is explained in many books and articles for the use among the laity, both Catholics and non-Catholics alike, to enhance their spiritual life. To learn more about Jesuits and the exercises, you may want to read the New York Times bestseller, *The Jesuit Guide to (Almost) Everything: A Spirituality of Real Life* by James Martin, S.J. (Harper Collins, 2010).

Back to the City of St. Francis: I knew that Santa Fe, New Mexico, is called the City of St. Francis, but why? Santa Fe means Holy Faith. I called my friend, Jane, in Santa Fe, who told me that when the Franciscans founded it, they called it, "the Royal Village of the Holy Faith of St. Francis of Assisi."

Since she would be there for Christmas, I told her I was coming to Santa Fe but had no idea why. All that I knew was that I had no choice but to obey the voice. With that trip, a whole new world opened up for me. God's presence was very real, very directive, and very decisive!

During the previous summer of 1990, a wonderful program in Retreat and Spiritual

Direction was being offered in Milford, Ohio, at a Jesuit retreat center. I had been thinking about leaving diocesan work and general Religious Education Ministry and to begin more studies in Spiritual Direction and Retreat Ministry. I believed that God was calling me to enter that program. I requested permission from my religious Community, and asked the Toledo diocese for two months off to do more study in these areas. The deadline was approaching fast, and the approval was coming slow. I was getting very impatient. How difficult it is to remember God's presence when life seems to stand still and answers are slow in coming! Finally, after several petitions to the Community, I was approved to study.

However, what I had in mind for me and what God had in mind for me were drastically, even dramatically, different. In just a few weeks, my life was thrown onto a totally new path, which in that moment in time was a mystery.

In early July, two weeks into the program, my brother called to tell me that Dad had had a stroke and was not expected to live the night. Leaving classes behind, I rushed home to Iowa, only to find that Dad was to linger for several more days. I was granted a gift, however, for I was able to stay with him on a cot in his room. About 3:00 A.M., we were both awake and alone and were able to have a wonderful visit.

When I awoke early the next morning, Dad was incoherent. The doctor said that he had done the best he could to save him, but his prognosis was nebulous. He could not predict how long Dad would live when both his body and mind were compromised—a week, a month, years?

I was being torn apart wishing to be with Dad, and at the same time wanting to continue the program. What difficult decisions we sometimes must make! At times such as these, I learned that God's presence is there but often too quiet to hear amidst my own distractions.

After several days of being in and out of the Milford program, and in conjunction with the director, I finally made the very difficult decision to leave. With no indication of Dad's imminent death, I went back to my diocesan work in Toledo. Several days later, Dad died.

After the funeral, my thoughts were troubled. "Should I go back to Milford the next summer? What should I be doing next? What did the future hold for me?" I wanted to move out of diocesan work and more into spirituality and accompany others on their spiritual journeys. I was also interested in doing retreat work.

Without warning, the dream answered my questions and confirmed the words I had heard at Mass, "Arlene, forget Milford and get yourself to Santa Fe."

Several days before Christmas, in a terrible snowstorm, I arrived in Santa Fe armed with names and places of Catholic parishes and the diocesan offices. I thought that perhaps I was to go back to working directly for the Church. I tried to be open to any and all possibilities. I just knew that I was no longer to work in the Toledo diocese, for new vistas were being opened up to me.

One day, my Santa Fe friend, Jane, said, "I think you should look at hospice."

My reply was quick and definite, "Jane, I am an educator, hospice is not for me."

A few days later, she repeated herself, and inside of me, I knew I could no longer negotiate or ignore the suggestion. Was God's presence manifested in her invitation? It seemed so! But would my religious Community support me in a totally new career when I was already in my fifties? They had already supported me for two Master's degrees. Would they be willing to pay for another degree, and an Associate's degree at that? It seemed very unlikely.

Yet, when I explained to my ministry director that I wanted to participate in a two-year program in the Elisabeth Kubler-Ross Institute in the tiny town of El Rito, New Mexico, she asked me one question: "What do you plan to do with that when you are finished?"

My answer came spontaneously, "I think I'd like to work in a mortuary." That reply was even a surprise to me!

I was shocked that the permission to move to New Mexico came so quickly and with so little dialogue, after all the problems I had just getting into a two-month program the summer before. In my life, all impediments seem to disintegrate when God makes His/Her presence and message known, and I am willing to respond. As I look back now, Milford was not for me, even though I loved the two weeks I was there. In New Mexico, everything fell into place. I knew that what I was to begin was the next phase of my life. My ministry director honored it and supported me. Again, I found that God participates in my life if only I listen and respond, even through a voice from within!

My ministry team, the Sisters with whom I lived, and other friends in Toledo, could not understand why I would leave a job I knew so well and start over in a city of which I knew nothing. I received all kinds of questions, comments, and loud messages that the move was too risky and that I was crazy. However, I was determined. I knew in my heart that it was right, and I was going to follow my heart.

What a turn my life took at that time! During the two years of study in Hospice, Grief Counseling, and Death Education, I learned about new cultures, new concepts, and various religious beliefs, the process of death and dying, not only in our own culture, but in other cultures in the United States and many from around the world. There was also a lot of discussion about what possibilities there may be of life after our life here on earth. The whole two-year study intrigued me.

After I finished the program, I moved to Santa Fe. As indicated in my dream, (and as I spontaneously told my ministry director, "I think I'd like to work in a mortuary,") I was hired by Beradinelli Family Funeral Service as a grief counselor. My ministry was to follow up with all the families who had lost a loved one, offer them individual counseling, and facilitate support groups. It was very significant to me to hear the owner, Rick Berardinelli, say to me upon hiring me, "I can no longer leave the grave site and see the pain people are in and not give them help."

I also taught credited classes in the community college, gave many talks and workshops, and directed retreats on the topics of grief and loss. As I created the ministry according to people's needs, I found that during those nearly twenty years, I served thousands of families. I was blessed with inspiration and wisdom from those who mourned their loved ones. As people moved through counseling, God's presence slowly became obvious to them, and appeared in abundant ways. What I learned during those years was more than I could ever have imagined when I first heard the voice telling me to go to Santa Fe.

Sometimes God calls us through a gentle whispering sound as He called Elijah in 1 Kings 19:11. For Elijah, God was not in the mighty wind, the earthquake, or the fire, but only in the whispering sound. Sometimes God calls us dramatically as He called Paul (Acts 9:3-9). And some of us, God must tell clearly what we are called to do, as in the call of Isaiah when God said, "Whom shall I send? Who will go? And Isaiah answered, "Here I am; send me" (Isaiah 6:8).

I had heard a call in a very different way and without knowing it, I had responded as did Isaiah, "Here I am; send me." I believe this was the most satisfying ministry I was ever called to do.

How does God call us? I learned many years ago from a very wise spiritual director that we need to recognize symbols, signs, and dreams, and to decode the messages and images that arise as we go about our daily tasks.

Are we all called? Yes! And to what are we called? I believe that we are ALL called to co-create in a positive way with the Divine. The messenger may be called our Higher Self, or the Higher Power, or a friend, or an inner voice. Or we may use another term that helps us to use our experiences to move us to greater good, greater service, and the ability to stand in a credible way before God, ourselves and others. Whichever term we use, God's guidance is always practical and calls us to a holier way of life.

My experience with that inner voice and the dream that followed several nights later told me so much about the presence of God in my life. Yet, as I remember so many other times, some of which are recorded in this book, it is so obvious that God's Presence is never far away. All those experiences are wonderful to contemplate when doubts come and feelings of discouragement are present.

The need is to listen to the gentle breeze or the loud message or the pain in my body or my dreams at night, or the shock to my psyche, or even the feeling that I live in confusion. Any or all of those experiences may indicate that God is giving me a message to join Him/Her in co-creating in a particular way.

As I learned how to listen and reflect more on these experiences, I recalled another message from many years ago. During the sixties and early seventies, many of our Sisters were leaving Communities. In fact, many of the sixty-five classmates who had entered Community with me, left. Priests were also leaving the orders and the dioceses.

My reflection and questions brought about thoughts of letting go of religious life. *Should I leave, too? I am still young. I can still build a fruitful life outside of a religious order —married or not. Maybe I made a mistake or perhaps this life is no longer for me and my journey is leading me elsewhere.* I had many questions but no answers!

One day, as I was contemplating this struggle, I distinctly heard a voice inside me, the exact words being, "Arlene, if I took care of you thus far, do you not think I will take care of you 'til the end?"

After that, I had no more doubts about leaving my religious community. Instinctively, I knew that the message was clear and that my path was to continue as a School Sister of St. Francis. Perhaps it was God's way of communicating that some of my work was to be a presence to others and to help them find the direction to God in their lives. Now in the evening of my life, that presence to God and others seems much more real and even more important. When we answer God's call, it seems that He takes us by the hand and works through us to help the people who are willing to respond to His love. We become God's messengers and communicators!

Over the years, I have counseled hundreds of people whom I met through the funeral home and in other ministries. I was always appreciative of the numbers of people who would make statements, such as, "Arlene, if it were not for you (or our support group) I would never have gotten through the pain of that death." Or, "you helped me find the right place for me." Or, "I have become stronger and no longer am an enabler to my alcoholic son (or husband)." Or, perhaps one of the best affirmations I heard was, "Arlene, you taught me how to meditate. I can now be more at peace with some of the physical problems that I have in my life." However, in my heart, I knew God was giving me the wisdom to say and do what was needed.

When people are hurting, the sincerity of their gratitude is amazing. One of the most gratifying times, however, is to be present with someone who has had an astounding breakthrough! When such people can face and overcome their difficult problems, they can take their reality to a new level. It is then that they gain a totally new awareness of themselves and the place of God in their lives.

One such experience happened several years ago. A woman whose second husband had died the previous year, responded to me for counseling through the funeral home after a second invitation. Over the course of several meetings, she told her horrendous story of terrible childhood abuse, as well as abuse from her first husband. She told me that the man, her second husband, who had died, was the only person who had ever really loved her. She was angry to a point of rage and trusted no one. One day, I said to her, "Healing is possible." I did not know it at the time, but that was a turning point in her life.

Several meetings later, I asked her why she had trusted me when she never trusted anyone in her life. Her answer amazed me.

She said, "Arlene, when you said to me that day, 'healing is possible,' I saw colors of electricity come out of your mouth. I went home and drew what I saw and placed it on my refrigerator. Every day, I would look at it and hope that it was true. I knew I could trust you and I knew you could help me." My prayer is that this woman continues to make strides in her journey toward the love that God is reaching out to her.

Another form of presence from the Spirit World that many people I have counseled experienced was the presence of their beloved after their death. These beloved include spouses, children, parents, friends, or even pets. Sometimes, people reported that when they spoke to their loved one, they got answers to the problems that were troubling them. As they talked to their loved one, things seemed to "fall into place" for them. Others saw them, felt them, heard them, or suddenly even smelled something that was pertinent only to the one on the other side. That was my experience many years after Mom had died.

At 3:30 one morning, I awoke suddenly and smelled freshly baked bread. I wondered, *Who on earth would be baking bread at that time in the morning?* I knew the people who lived around me and was sure it was no one in the apartment building. Then I felt my Mom's presence. As a child, I saw Mom baking bread, sweet rolls, pies, and all kinds of other tasty treats several times a week. She was a great baker! When I woke that morning and smelled bread baking, I was sure she was letting me know she was around. The fragrance lasted for just a few moments and then was gone. I felt a joy to know that she was present!

Another experience was a very real dream about my sister and I knew she, too, had been present in that dream. I woke up saying aloud, "Ethel, it was so good to see you again."

The more I worked with children, particularly little ones, I found that they often had an uncanny connection with a parent, grandparent, or even a pet who has died. Three-year-old Kristine kept telling her grandmother that her "Bampa (Grandpa) was here." She described him as playing with her and her brother and being present many times. Kristine's grandmother never discouraged her, but was not too sure just what was going on. In fact, she was quite doubtful of the whole situation.

One day, Kristine said, "Grandma, Bampa had a different shirt on today." When Rita, her grandmother, questioned her as to what kind of shirt he had on, Kristine described a favorite shirt that he had worn before Kristine was born. Kristine had never seen the shirt. Because of her grandfather's illness, the shirt no longer fit and had been put aside. The doubter became a believer that day!

It seemed to me that the grandfather wanted his wife to believe their grandchild and that his presence was real. Our departed loved ones do not just abandon us. Their presence is with us, and if we are open to them, we may still interact with them.

While I worked at Berardinelli Family Funeral Service, the doctrine in the Creed, which Catholics and many other Christians say each Sunday, "I believe in the Communion of Saints," became much more alive within me. After many of my own experiences and the conversations I had with others, that doctrine became very real. It is no longer only something that I believe; it has become something that I know to be true.

One other powerful story showing the power of God's presence took place while I was in leadership in our religious Community. We have School Sisters of St. Francis in Peru, and Joan, whom I know well, and who was a missionary, asked me to come to Peru to visit them to better understand their work.

The day I was to leave Peru and return to home, the pastor gave me a large check (obtained from the German bishops) to purchase a car for the Sisters and a truck for the parish. I was shocked and frightened, since I was to visit two other Latin American countries. *How could I protect that money until I got home and get it into the bank? What a responsibility!* I needed to trust God's presence to take over.

Finally, when the money was safe, I took a trip to Calmar, Iowa, a small town where I had worked many years prior. I approached a Ford dealer whose son I had taught in high school and knew well. When I asked him to help me obtain these vehicles for Peru, he thought I was kidding. He knew it would be a big job, but after convincing him that I was serious, he said that he would work with me.

I did not want him to do it for free, and in his generosity, he said that he would take $100 per vehicle (which was nothing). Later, he called me to say that he forgot to have a hitch put on the truck for towing. He would use the $200 to make sure there was a hitch on the truck. I mention his generosity because after the cars were safely in Peru, his wife told me that "my" vehicles gave her husband the necessary sold quota. The Ford

Company gave him a trip to Omaha, where he won $2,000 at the horse races. God's gift for generosity!

As we worked to get the cars to Peru and what that would cost, questions arose loud and clear. I also became more worried when people began to tell me that other groups had tires stolen, wheels removed, and a multitude of other problems. 1 must admit that I never prayed so hard. I talked to God constantly to get the cars to Peru safely.

Then one day, Joan called from Peru. She said, "Arlene, I was on the streets of Paita today and I met a man from the Caribbean Transit Authority. I asked him about getting the cars to Paita, which is a small port. When I told him what they were to be used for, he said, 'Well, space available—nothing'." Wow!

Many of my fears disappeared, and even though much had to be done and many calls made to this man, it was not long before Joan called at 3:30 A.M. and shouted into the phone, "Arlene, the cars are here, and they are in perfect condition."

Prayer, and sorry to say, worry and stewing, seem to get lots of God's attention. This was a true realization of God's presence in my life and I am forever grateful. Many years later, the Sisters' car is still working.

In this chapter, I tried to show the movement from finding the presence of God in our own lives to being the presence of God in another person's life. I have also found that in being that presence to another can be costly.

If I try to do the work alone without God's presence, if I forget to "protect" myself with the Light of Christ, I quickly lose energy and feel myself getting drained. Sometimes, when I work with certain people, they literally sap my energy. The person may come into my office filled with anger or rage or be filled with other emotions that caused their energy to wane. They, then, unconsciously would take mine.

Many readers may not be aware of this phenomenon, but my experience and the experience of others who are aware of the movement of energy, have shared their experiences with me.

After a counseling session, I may become very fatigued and drained. It is then that I realize too late that I tried to do the work by myself. My mentor, Robert Waterman, often told me that God's job is 90 percent and that my job is only 10 percent. However, I must do my 10 percent, 100 percent of the time.

When I try to be a real presence to another who is in deep pain, I have learned how important it is to be aware of the energy in my own body and to keep it connected to the Divine. It is important to be a witness to the feelings and pain of another, but not to take them into our being. Our presence will be more healing and open when our energy is steeped in the Christ or God energy.

REFLECTION

As you check into the Divine Presence in your life, take some time for silence and deep breathing. Focus on your energy. Do you feel drained? Fatigued? Where does the lack of energy manifest itself in your body? Where do you feel tension? Where is that tension coming from? Does it arise from stress or burnout, or depression, or not sleeping the night before?

Do you feel discomfort or pain in the body? Does it come from emotions that have not been cleared? Are you finding it difficult working with people who have many problems? It may even be coming from the energies in the planet that affect us all—the anger, violence, hatred, war, injustice, greed, and in general, the pain within our planet. Any of those experiences may have drained away your energy. It is important to recognize whether the fatigue, tenseness or lack of energy is ours or whether it comes from an outside source.

SUGGESTION

As you check into your own energy, invite the Light, the Christ/God energy, the presence of the Divine, into your feelings. You may wish to invite others from the Spirit World, such as healers, teachers, angels, and beings of Light who are willing to be present and to extend their loving presence and gifts of grace into your life. I find that the Spirit World is very near and inviting Spirits into my life has eased tensions in my body many times.

WRITING OPTION

What? Write about a time when you felt the presence of someone who has passed. What happened when you felt this way? Were you seeking guidance or under duress at the time, or did the presence of the departed enter into your awareness by surprise? Who was it? Why do you think s/he visited you?

If you have not felt the presence of someone who has passed, you might write about someone important and meaningful in your life (a mentor or parent) who in a time of need was there for you even though s/he was not actually physically present.

You may also have felt the presence of Christ, God, Mary, saints, angels, or other spiritual or religious being. Write about those special experiences and what happened when you felt that presence.

So What? Why was the presence of this person or spiritual being so important or meaningful for you? What did her/his presence help you accomplish or overcome? How did the presence make you feel? If you felt sad or scared, why do you think you felt this way? If you felt happy, why do you think you felt this way? Reflecting now on the incident, how do you feel about it today?

Now What? As you move forward with your spiritual journey, write about how you plan to open yourself up to the Divine Presence and attempt to develop into a higher self that is in tune with and welcome to the energies of others. How do you plan to be present for others? How do you plan to use the Christ/God's Light to help you help others? What do you think you might learn and experience from this potentially new direction in your spiritual life?

Chapter 8

CREATIVITY

Let the children come to me.
Do not hinder them. The kingdom of God
belongs to such as these.
And He laid His hands on their heads
before He left that place.
(Matthew 19:14-15)

"We need a Dougy Center in Santa Fe." I woke up to these words one morning early in 1997.

I had been working in the funeral home for several years and 1996 had been a terrible year for the deaths of children—mostly teenagers. It was heart-rending to bury three teenagers in three months within the same family. A set of seventeen-year-old twins was killed in an accident on May 2, and their sister died in an accident in late July. This mother lost all three of her children in three months after just sustaining a difficult divorce. What a tragedy! How could she ever endure this pain and begin to heal after such a terrible experience? At another time, our funeral home held the bodies of three teenagers killed together in another accident.

Through the years as I worked as a grief counselor at Berardinelli's, there were many accidents, numerous suicides and murders, as well as so many natural deaths, which affected our children. It overwhelmed me to see these young people dying and to see their families, friends, and classmates without any support to help the survivors grieve.

As we buried children, parents, grandparents, and close friends of the children and teens of Santa Fe, I also worried about the children who survived. I asked myself many questions. *How would they grieve their losses? How could they be helped to find some sort of solace? Would they turn to unhealthy behavior as they attempted to move on with life? What do we need in Santa Fe to help them? As the grief counselor in this funeral home, what could I do?*

There was just no place in Santa Fe supporting the grief of children! On some level, I "knew" I would have to establish one. The answer came as I awoke that morning hearing the voice: "We need a Dougy Center in Santa Fe." The words came spontaneously with no warning.

I had heard about the Dougy Center (named after, Douglas, a child dying of cancer) from the textbook I was using when I taught a course on Death and Dying in the community college. A nurse in Portland, Oregon had discovered that a dying child could intuit how to help another child die. She concluded that if children could help each other die, they could also help each other grieve. Thus, the "Dougy Center" was created. It was based upon the philosophy of children helping children.

Volunteer adults facilitate support groups according to age and work with groups of children from three to eighteen. They use discussion, play, art, exercise, and any medium that will help the child move through the pain and process of grief, including a safe "Tornado Room" to encourage the children to move through the anger they feel at such a time.

During that time, another facilitator works with the adults who brought each child to the Center. The program sounded like something that I needed to look into, to see if it fit the community of Santa Fe, New Mexico.

I obtained material from Portland and presented it to the support group, which I had been facilitating for parents who had lost their children. Imagine my surprise when five parents immediately volunteered to go with me to attend the training in Portland! In a couple of weeks, two other interested women joined us. Another surprise came when several people and a few groups in the Santa Fe community were willing to trust our endeavor. Their generosity provided us with the needed money to attend the week-long training in Portland—another experience of God's presence. The training was an amazing new experience for all of us, and we returned well equipped to help children and families grieve the death of a loved one. Our work was cut out for us!

We were committed to establishing a center in Santa Fe to support children whose lives had been torn apart. Our needs were great. We needed a board, a 501c3 for tax purposes, a logo for advertising to let the community know of our work, a director, a name, a place to gather the children and adults for support groups, toys, furniture, AND we needed money.

This was certainly a new venture, and it was overwhelming. But I was not alone! Eight of us had gone to Portland, and we had returned well-trained and inspired; our work was difficult, but we accomplished it. The center became known as Gerard's House, after a teenager who had been killed in an accident while traveling to Denver. The work with children who were grieving was underway!

Establishing a non-profit organization—finding space, money, equipment, furniture, and especially working with the IRS—is not an easy task. Nor was it easy to be the board, become the first facilitators, train new adults to take over as facilitators, and to try to keep all those relationships from total breakdown.

There were many bumps along the way, and several times, I was tempted to give up.

However, this was God's project, and S/He would not let that happen. God always came through with new people to help facilitate, the gifts of furniture and toys, many items needed for the children and of course, money. I also had the support of wonderful friends who encouraged me and stuck with me through the pain of a very new beginning. Surely, this was another example in my life that told me that when God wants something to happen, things will fall into place. God will not be outdone in generosity. It was right, and God was truly in our midst! After all these years, Gerard's House is still functioning well in Santa Fe, and has served more than 4,000 children.

I entitled this chapter, "Creativity." For most people, creativity means the creation of a beautiful painting, sculpture, weaving, or any wonderful piece of art produced by persons with artistic talent. When the word creativity is mentioned, images of various talented musicians, dancers, the beauty of ballet, the excitement of the theater, and any other creation that excites the person's sense of beauty comes to mind.

I learned to appreciate this sense of beauty in music and art since many School Sisters of St. Francis excelled in those gifts. As a young Sister, we attended many concerts given by our Sisters and saw much art produced by them. Our exquisite chapel, St. Joseph's in Milwaukee, Wisconsin, speaks to that interest and that beauty. I, however, did not have those talents, so I needed to learn to appreciate them in others.

It is said that all children are artists. Yet, as a child in school, any art assignments were painful to me, and my mother was neither affirming nor encouraging. As I mentioned in an earlier chapter, Mom was an excellent pianist, knowing how to play both by ear and by notes. We girls took music lessons, but none of us could compare to Mom's artistic ability. As for art, if it did not look realistic, her comments were negative. Consequently, I grew up never thinking I had the ability to be creative.

For many years, I admired these works of art, as I did not possess any of the talents mentioned above, I never thought of myself as creative. However, when I began to look over the experiences of teaching, facilitating workshops and support groups, conducting retreats, counseling, and other means of being present to people, I realized how much creative work went into the preparation and the carrying out of those activities. So as I finished the extensive project of leading the creation of Gerard's House, I knew that with God, my work could also be termed "creative." The Dougy Center in Portland, Oregon, was creatively adapted to Gerard's House in Santa Fe, where many people speak Spanish.

I now view creativity as anything we do that adapts a pre-established form to meet the unique needs of those served. There are times when pre-established forms and structure must be followed for work to get done smoothly. However, it is much more exciting, and often more helpful for others, if we find our own creative expression in the performance of our work.

A boss, a leader, or a parent has the potential to develop within us an appreciation for creativity or to stifle it. They also have the ability to help us admire the beauty of the arts, as well as our own creative works. It was my religious Community that instilled the love of music and art in me, but it was individual Sisters who taught me to recognize my own ability when I began teaching early on in my career.

Over the years, I have been with principals and other leaders who have suggested a project to complete, explaining the final goal to accomplish, yet have given me and my peers freedom to complete it in the way that used our own abilities to fulfill it. Those were the persons in my life who helped me to become creative. As a young, beginning teacher, the best principal I had was Sister Judea. She was the person who gave me the guidance I needed and supported me in the ideas I had for my classroom. She encouraged my own inspiration and awareness of the power that I had within, and she presented me with the opportunity to become a very good teacher.

As noted earlier in this book (Chapter 3), I had spent my novitiate praying, "God, send me anywhere but not to Chicago." Guess what? My first assignment after novitiate was to St. William's in Chicago to teach second grade. Both the parish and the school were large. I was assigned to one of two class-rooms in which I was to teach (or try to teach) fifty-four squirmy second graders. I must admit, the first year was disastrous, but I learned quickly and the next year was much better. Sister Judea arrived the third year and it was wonderful to have her as a principal for six years. By that time, I had learned much and her support was invaluable.

Because registration was so high in those days, real creativity was a must. There was no aide. I was it!

I divided the class into five small reading groups according to ability. I taught one small group in the front of the room (to see what was going on); two groups of children were in the corners of the room, reading aloud to each other. One group was at the table, being "taught" by a brighter student, using material that I had given them; and the members of another group were in their seats doing what we called "seatwork." After twenty minutes or so, I would call the children to attention and everyone would move to a new place until all five groups had a chance in each section.

When Sister Judea came into the room, she marveled and praised my system as she saw the children learn. As the years went on, my classroom was used as a model for teachers in the Archdiocese of Chicago. St. Williams was a real laboratory for creative teaching for me. I learned to love the city and was grateful to have been assigned to Chicago.

I believe that Sister Judea's leadership gave me the courage to assume the leadership that I took on many times later in my life. I felt that she trusted me and that trust on the part of leadership made me more secure within myself and taught me about my own gifts and abilities. It enhanced my highest good, as well as the highest good of the children in my classroom.

If prohibited from using our creative abilities, we become robots, doing our jobs with no ingenuity. This usually destroys any creative expression. These are the times when most of us become bored and do the job poorly, just to get it done. If we must do a certain job, which takes little or no creativity, I believe that we must find other outlets, such as a hobby—painting, woodworking, sports, piano, classes, or some other kind of creative experience.

Creativity, of course, can be used for wrong-doing. A bank robber may be creative in robbing a bank, or a dishonest person may "creatively" figure out how to fraudulently cheat another person or institution. Consider for a moment the creativity it took to "create" the weaponry, biological or other types of weapons, present in our world. Think for another moment the horrors "creatively" committed in wars and the mistreatment of people by those who hate, seek revenge, and who live in fear. Persons of different orientations, different ethnic or religious groups, different nationalities or cultures are subject to judgment, and therefore, it is considered to be right to "creatively" find ways to harm, get rid of, punish, or torture them. We consider them "the others."

Rather than using creativity to do harm, I am stressing creativity in this chapter to be thought of only as an enhancement of the person's highest good.

The job of good leadership, therefore, is to bring out people's good and creative energies. Inspiration and encouragement are very important. To stifle a person who shows signs of creativity is harmful to the person, and to the institution or organization. A real leader recognizes that it takes a lot of creativity to cook a delicious meal, renovate an old building, write an essay, swim or play any kind of sport. Even cleaning out a cupboard and organizing the contents, or setting up a house after moving can be a way to use the creativity that resides within each of us.

Certainly, starting Gerard's House was a call to creativity. As I look back now, I drew on more creativity within me than I realized I possessed. Yes, I had to be creative in order to help the community of Santa Fe. This creative energy can flourish and increase through other imaginative people giving new and different perspectives to challenges in our lives. Thus, the creative person can aspire to touch others through her work, or the activity she performs, simple though it may be.

How can anyone think about creativity, however, without thinking of the Master Creator? St. Thomas Aquinas, who lived centuries ago, said, "God is an artist and the universe is God's work of art." The Book of Genesis describes in a mythological way how the universe and this planet were created. In the simplicity of the story, Genesis recounts the darkness being filled with Light, the spinning into reality of the sun, the moon, and the stars, the fashioning of the seas, and the method used to form the land. It explains the techniques that God used to create the water creatures and the animals. Finally, human beings were uniquely formed and entered into this magical earth.

The author of the story himself was extremely creative. The story form in the Book of Genesis recording God's artistry is both a creative work on the part of the author telling this imaginative story, and a magnificent portrayal of the God who created this beautiful planet: "And God looked upon all that (he) had made and saw that it was good" (Genesis, 1:31).

Matthew Fox, in his beautiful book, *Creativity: Where the Divine and the Human*

Meet, (Penguin Putnam, Inc., 2002) entitles a chapter, "Creativity, Our True Nature." In that chapter, he explains that we are creators at our very core. And that only by creating can we be truly happy. As we create, we touch the very deepest powers of ourselves and the Divine, he writes. Quoting Fox on page 28, we read, "When the Bible declares that we are made in the 'image and likeness' of the Creator, it is affirming that creativity is at our core just as it lies at the core of the Creator of all things." In reality, then, we really become co-creators with the Divine. To emphasize this point, Fox quotes the Sufi mystic, Hafiz, who writes in one of his poems

> *All the talents of God are within you.*
> *How could this be otherwise*
> *When your soul*
> *derived from His genes!*

Thus, creativity is not only music or art or dance. Creativity is whatever we do that gives meaning to our lives. It is the stuff of our creations that draws us closer to being co-creators with the Divine. This kind of creativity will help us as we seek our highest good in all that we do.

REFLECTION

Again, move into a silent space. Quiet music may be played. Breathe deeply, inviting your own creativity into your meditation. Look at the career, the job, or the volunteer work that you have done in your life. Note how much creative work you have already accomplished. Honor yourself for that job well done.

Have you been forced to be a robot in your work? Have your ideas been thwarted or ignored by a boss, only to be used by him or her later claiming it as his or her own? What does that do to you? Are you able to challenge him or her as you speak your truth about the situation?

SUGGESTION

Recognize how our Creator has directed your creativity as you began something new or different or difficult. Honor yourself for following your activity or a new beginning. Thank God for the direction given you from above. If someone has misused your creative ideas, spend some time to become aware of your feelings, and if possible, let them go; if it is not too soon, try to forgive that person.

WRITING OPTION

What? Write about a time when you used your creative energy to compose something—a poem, a story, a painting, a song. What did you do? Why did you create that thing? What was the outcome and what impact did your creation have on other people? On you? You may also write about something you composed that falls outside the traditional concepts of "creativity."

As I explained in this chapter, creativity stretches in all directions as an outpouring of spiritual energy from the Divine. So your creation might also be a particularly clever idea you had at home for overcoming a challenge so that some task might be accomplished. As a creative idea you had might involve a nifty fix for some plumbing or having students write a grant proposal to help a neighborhood build a playground. Or it might even involve a creative approach to solving a pesky problem at work that is keeping your organization from flourishing.

So What? Why is this particular creative endeavor so important to you? Why does it hold so much meaning? Why did this incident pop into your mind, and how does it make you feel now when you reflect back on it?

What Now? Write about your plans for enriching or continuing your creativity. What are some concrete steps that you can take to tap into that creativity to help spread that positive energy to others? How can you share the thrill and generative spirit that creativity sparks with people who might not have been exposed to these things?

If you haven't been creative in a while, write about what you need to do in order to spark your creative energy. Do you need a break from the busy routine of life to create? Or are you most creative when you are in the midst of the hustle and bustle of a chaotic life? Have you always wanted to take a painting class? Write about what you need to do to accomplish that. Have you always wanted to be more involved in your community's work to help solve local problems? Write about what steps you need to take to become more involved so that you can add your creative energy and co-create with the Divine and other creative mystics to help bring about positive change.

Chapter 9

HEALING

He heals the broken hearted
And binds up their wounds.
(Psalm 147:3)

"People don't want to listen to my story anymore, but I need to tell my story, until I don't have to tell it anymore." (*A mother whose husband was killed by a drive-by shooter*)

"My sister died at twelve when I was six. My parents were so absorbed in her death, that I felt abandoned, alienated, and isolated. Now as an adult, it is telling on my family." (*A woman with husband and children*)

"My baby was two years old when my sister ran over him

with a car. I could never talk about it because I did not want to hurt my sister's feelings. Now I can." (*A 70-plus-year-old woman in a support group*)

"I just miss them. I just miss them." (*A mother who lost all three of her teenage children through accidents in three months*)

"And two angels swooped down and picked him up and disappeared!" (*A twelve-year-old boy during a counseling session who had been on the verge of suicide after the death of his best friend*)

"I would like to go on with my life, but I do not know if my wife would approve." (*A husband many months after the death of his wife*) rief is hard, and pain affects us all when death or other tragedies enter our lives. But we all want to be healed, and we all need to be healed, whether it is in this life or seemingly also in the next.

I was given the opportunity to find that out a few years ago. Louise has given me permission to relate an astounding story about her husband who had died about two years previous to this experience.

I got to know Louise in a very interesting way—which tells me that this story was being guided from the other side.

I conducted a grief support group for the Cathedral in Santa Fe, New Mexico, every Tuesday night for some years. One Sunday, after Mass, as I went to receive and take the Eucharist to a homebound client, Father Jerome, the Rector of the Cathedral, told the Congregation that if any were in need of a support group for grief, one was available on Tuesday night. Never before nor after did he make that announcement.

Louise was the first one there, and after asking her name and who had died, she volunteered that she really lived in Durango,

Colorado. After telling me that she and her husband, Richard, had lived and worked in Chicago for most of their lives together, she volunteered that she had grown up in Iowa.

"Oh, where?" I asked.

"Oh, you probably never heard of it."

"Try me," I countered. I know Iowa.

"Waukon", she answered.

"Oh, that is about forty miles from where I grew up," I responded with a smile.

She was familiar with Fort Atkinson and the St. Anthony Chapel, which belongs to our family. When I asked her maiden name, I said, "We're related!" We figured out that her great-grandmother and my grandmother were sisters. Louise and I were cousins!

Another person, Marjorie, also came to the group that night. Marjorie had lost her son, her husband, and her mother—all from cancer—in the course of two years and was filled with grief. The three of us eventually became good friends.

A few years later, I retired and moved back to Milwaukee where I would be closer to the School Sisters of St. Francis. The three of us kept in touch—Marjorie in Santa Fe,

Louise in Durango, and me in Milwaukee. In July of that year, Louise and Marjorie came for a visit. While here, Louise encouraged me to come to Durango to see where she lived. I hesitated. After all, they were just here! We had just spent several days having a wonderful visit and sightseeing in Milwaukee. Louise was very insistent. She offered to pay my way if I would come. She really wanted me to see her home in the mountains. So finally, I said I would travel to Durango. In August, I flew into Albuquerque, Marjorie picked me up, and together, we drove to Durango.

When I entered her beautiful home in the mountains, I felt Richard's energy very strongly. Richard had died in that house! His presence was still very alive there.

Louise told us the story of his death in their house. On a morning when Louise had an appointment, Richard was not feeling well. Their mountain home was about a half a mile to the highway. She told him that when she got to the highway, she would call to see how he was. When she called, he said that he was no better. She told him she would turn around, come back, and call 911.

When she arrived the ambulance was already there, and the medics were trying to revive him. Richard had been a very strong Catholic, but there was no time to have him anointed. He had died very suddenly.

One morning, while Louise was making breakfast and the three of us were visiting, I began to tell a story of an experience several years before. In it, I mentioned the word *anointing.* Louise immediately said, "Richard wants to be anointed."

I thought, "How will I do that?" Yet, I knew exactly what to do. (I have carried specially blessed oil in my purse for many years.)

"Louise," I said, "I will use your body as a proxy. I will anoint your forehead, your heart, your hands, and your feet." So as the three of us, Louise, Marjorie, and I, gathered around the table, I proceeded to anoint her body as Richard's proxy, making up prayers as I did so. As I was finished, I looked at Marjorie, who was crying.

When I asked if she was OK, she said, "I *SAW* him. He came in, walked around the table, put his hands on Louise's shoulder, and when you anointed her (his) feet, he turned into Light and disappeared."

Wow! Now all of us were in tears. Was it truly Richard? When Marjorie described what she saw, Louise laughed. He had on long sleeves, yes, that was what he always wore. Then Marjorie said that he had on a large, oval, silver belt buckle. Louise told the story that when they moved to Colorado, he always wanted a large, oval, silver belt buckle, but could only find a square one. Now, on the other side, he had his wish—a large, oval, silver belt buckle!

I truly believe that it was Richard and that he wished to be anointed to be at peace and move into the Light. He then could be with her in a new and helpful way.

I also am convinced that Richard orchestrated the whole plan. Why had Louise come down to Santa Fe at the invitation of friends a few months after Richard's death? Why was she in the cathedral at that particular Mass on that particular Sunday when Father Jerome made the announcement? Why was she so driven to attend my support group when she would be going back to Durango in a few days and perhaps not be able to attend regularly? She had no idea who I was.

My belief is that Richard knew that I would not be intimidated and would find a way to carry out his desire. Mystery? There were many mysteries I encountered as I worked with so many people in grief. My ministry in the funeral home as a grief counselor had been full of mysteries. I deem it to be the best ministry of my life.

So how did I try to help those who were in grief or tragedy?

As I mentioned before, everything fell into place when I finally got to New Mexico. I had listened to the voice and believed the dream. I had worked through my denial about hospice and finally surrendered when my Community supported me. God was certainly directing me, and I could no longer doubt.

As mentioned above, I took two years of classes in hospice, grief counseling, and death education following the Elisabeth Kubler-Ross program in that little New Mexican town, El Rito. The classes were filled with new ideas and information and studies that I had never before encountered. We learned about the history of hospice, starting with the monks in the early centuries, and how hospice is done in our own times. We learned how to counsel people in grief, and the way many other peoples around the world understood death and worked through it. We also learned the Western way of healing and many alternatives as practiced in the East.

Because I had been a teacher all my life, I was asked to teach a few of the classes after I had taken them myself. Those two years opened a whole new world for me and I have been changed forever!

When I teach Death Education, I use a motto that I think is helpful: *Grief is not a problem to be solved; rather it is a process whereby we can choose to integrate it into our lives, thereby becoming a healthier and holier person.*

I tried to be aware of this as I counseled, remembering that it is a process. Everyone grieves differently. Everyone grieves at his or her own pace. Everyone has many feelings to express as he or she faces the reality of major changes. No one can say when his or her grief is over. In a sense, it may never be. However, moving through the process usually helps people receive the strength to go on with life, whether it is finding a new and different life or enhancing the present one.

A priest mentioned how much I had changed after my back surgeries. People who suffer can use their pain for growth and compassion. I told my second graders after being hurt on the playground that they could become bitter or better. This same idea holds true for adults when they suffer loss.

As I listened to people speak about grief, I often hear them express Elisabeth Kubler-Ross' five stages of grief: Denial, Bargaining, Anger, Depression, Acceptance. She recorded those stages as she was working with the dying, not as she worked with people in grief. I found this process difficult to transfer into the process of grief.

I found the system of J. William Worden taken from his book, *Grief Counseling and Grief Therapy: A Handbook for the Mental Health Practitioner* (Second Edition, 1991), much more helpful and appropriate as I dealt with the grieving person. Worden discusses four tasks of mourning. I mention them here with a little explanation, since they may be helpful to any reader who may be in grief or supporting someone who is. Worden, however, goes into much more detail and I encourage any interested reader to make use of his wisdom.

Task One: *To accept the reality of the loss.* The person needs to hear harsh words, such as dead, death, mortuary, funeral, gravesite, and the fact that the person will not return in this lifetime (physical reality). It is important to use such words gently, rather than "asleep" or "gone," especially among children who may assume that the person will wake up or come back as from a trip. However, even adults need these words to hold back the temptation to deny the reality of the death of their loved one.

Task Two: *To work through the pain of grief.* Sadness, guilt, fear, feeling overwhelmed, powerlessness, despair, and always anger— with God, the person who died, the situation, or self, and many other feelings that rise up in grieving people. The person may feel all of the above at one time, and needs to be helped to separate them so that they can slowly be identified and healed. I once heard a person say, "I'm so damned mad at him for dying and leaving me in this mess." All feelings are honest for the grieving person even though they make no sense to others.

Task Three: *To adjust to an environment in which the deceased is missing.* As time moves on, the grieving person will slowly face the reality of the death, and will come to a new identity of self without the parent, the spouse, the child, the wonderful friend or even the pet. Hopefully there is support, through friends, a grief support group, a counselor, and/or family, so that the grieving person will begin to face new challenges and situations that will begin and continue the healing process.

Task Four: *To emotionally relocate the deceased and move on with life.* During this last task, the grieving person, if not stuck, will search for new opportunities. If the loss was a spouse, a younger person may choose to go back to school, find a different job, build new friendships or choose to move into a new relationship or remarry. Older people may have to make difficult choices, such as selling the house, moving in with children, or a facility whereby they will feel safe. They too, need the support of family and friends and/or support groups. Each must find what they need so that healing can take place.

~ ~ ~ ~ ~

I made a point above to mention "choice." I have counseled people who actually chose to be a "victim" and were not interested in moving on with life even after several years. It is very difficult to encourage people who make the choice to refuse to choose a path of healing. Prayer for that person seems to be the only way.

As I worked with people in grief, I found that many other losses that people experienced besides death needed the same process: the loss of precious objects, such as a wedding ring, a wrecked car, a flooded or burned out house, or other items. Other situations, which are important to a person's life, such as financial difficulties, also need this process. The loss of one's health, whether it is sudden or through a serious illness, the loss of a limb, eyesight, hearing, and any other health issue are very serious losses that must be grieved.

Many years ago, a woman asked if she would fit into a retreat on grief that I was offering. She had been abused by her father and "lost her childhood." Definitely a major loss, as is domestic violence! And as we move through our lives major changes occur. These changes also need to be grieved.

With any serious loss, our whole being is affected—physically, emotionally, mentally, socially, and spiritually, and we suffer feelings and notice behaviors that are totally new to the griever. It is important that each one take notice of the sensations that occur within, face that reality and talk to friends, or a counselor, and pray if possible. I say "if possible" because often grieving people are angry at God. *Why? Why? Why? Why did a "merciful God" let this happen?* God understands that anger and continues to love. God is still present, even though S/He seems absent.

In the wonderful poem, *Footprints in the Sand*, author Mary Stevenson in a dream walks with God on the beach. She notices that there are two set of footprints, and realizes that God walked with her throughout his life. Then she noticed only one set. "Why, God, when I needed you most, were you absent?" God answered, "My precious child, I love you and I would never leave you. During times of trials and suffering, when you see only one set of footprints, it was then that I carried you." I invite us all to remember this poem when pain enters into our lives.

There is so much to understand about the grieving process. The age of the person, the sex, the personality, the religion, the nationality, other stresses in the person's life, and the amount of support available all needs to be assessed. In many tragedies, it may be that counseling is imperative, especially if the grief is more complicated.

As a friend, how can you help the person who experienced a tragedy? I would like to suggest several ideas. First of all, it is important to support the person in his/her own process. As mentioned, everyone grieves differently and at his or her own pace. That needs to be recognized and supported and never pushed in "normal" grieving. Words usually do not help much, but hugs and presence usually do.

If the loss is a death, offer to take care of children, pick someone up from the airport, bring food, offer to stay in the house during the funeral if the neighborhood does not seem safe or just ask someone what needs to be done.

It is important to keep the person attuned to the reality of the death. As mentioned above, when dealing with children, it is not wise to use "sleep" rather than "death" or to use words that cover up the reality. It is helpful to take the child, even small children, to the wake, but never without explanation and answering the child's questions. Children's imaginations are very alive, and they need to be comforted and included by the adults around them, as well as feeling part of the sad experience. A child may play one minute and cry the next, and needs to know that is OK.

One night at Berardinelli Family Funeral Service, a beautiful three-year-old child was in the casket. His parents asked me if his six-year-old sister should be taken in to see him. I knelt down so as to face the child directly as she sat on her father's lap. I then explained that her little brother would not be able to play with her, that he would feel hard and not smile. He could not look at her. I asked the father to carry her in, with me accompanying them. The little girl looked at her brother and reached out to touch him. I stopped her, reiterating that he would not feel soft and he would not respond. She then touched him and she seemed OK, at least for the time being.

I often told people to "feel the feelings," to identify them, to separate them—from fear to guilt to anger to helplessness. A friend can help them to do so, as well as to be present when the person is beginning to suffer from being alone. Each person needs plenty of time to grieve and to cry and to learn to laugh again. Patience on the part of friends is very helpful as is support throughout the entire process.

I stress again, in the Christian Creed, there is a phrase, "I believe in the Communion of Saints." That belief became very alive to me as I was working in Bernardinelli's dealing daily with grieving people.

Two more stories seem to fit here which show how we, on earth, have a strong connection with the other side .... another proof of the Communion of Saints.

One morning, a friend of mine, Marjorie, was meditating. Her son had died and her grief was still raw. Suddenly, she saw him. He had been devastated by cancer, including having lost his arm. In her vision, she saw him totally healed. His face was radiant. His chest began to glow. He had become whole. She was able to move with him as they moved toward the Light. Then she knew she could go no further.

As Marjorie stepped back, she saw what looked like tiles falling from him. She understood those tiles to mean: *I don't need to finish college. I don't need to become an optometrist. I don't need to marry my fiancée. I don't need to have children. I just need to go to the Light.* That vision was most comforting to his mother, whose grief had been so intense.

Visions do not keep back the tears of loss, but they give us the assurance that life on the other side is real and our loved ones are happy and secure.

The other unique story connecting the living on this side with the living on the other side took place at the bedside of a dying priest friend. I had worked with this priest, Gerald, for seven years. During the last few years, before I left the parish, his cancer had returned. As Gerald grew more and more ill, he and his housekeeper moved out of the parish and Gerald was eventually moved into a home for the aged.

Since my parents lived nearby, I often visited him. My home was in Des Moines, Iowa, at that time—about a three-and-a-half-hour drive. One weekend, I planned to visit, but had had a small accident the week before. Plans changed, but as I sat down to pray on Friday morning, I suddenly realized that I was pulling my suitcase off the shelf. "I guess I am supposed to go to see Gerald," I mused.

I left about 2:00 P.M. and arrived around 5:30. Florence, his housekeeper, was surprised to see me and asked what I was doing there.

I replied, "I don't know."

Fifteen minutes later, we were called to Gerald's bedside at a retirement center in another town, about a ten-minute drive away.

Florence had never driven in her life, so when the call came, I was available.

Gerald had a great devotion to Mary, the Mother of Jesus. This was shown in his praying the rosary each day before Mass. (The rosary is a special devotion used by Catholics, which has been said for centuries.) When we arrived, I asked if he wished to say the rosary.

"No. Too long," he said. Gerard was extremely weak since the cancer had destroyed his body. His mind, however, was totally clear.

Florence and I stood vigil, saying short prayers and holding his hand. Another dear friend arrived and the three of us women watched and prayed.

Suddenly, without warning, and not looking at the three of us, he sat up in bed, reached out his arms and said, "Help me!"

After a few short breaths, he was gone. I have no doubt that he saw Mary, the Mother of Jesus. She had come to welcome her devoted son to the other side. The next day, December 8, was one of her special feast days!

I have told many stories throughout this book, of experiences I had, as well as relating the stories of many other people whom I have known and cared about. Those stories were precious to the individual and very helpful. Imagination? Sometimes, maybe, but if the person who died is felt by the survivor, that presence, even in imagination, has helped the person to accept the loss. In that case, imagination is helpful.

I know for certain that the Spirit World is very much present. The Spirits are around us and are able to support us. They are interested in what we do and many times serve as a guide in our needs. When I sat down to write this book, I asked for help from anyone in the Spirit World to be present and help if he or she chose to do so. Often, I got inspiration or a suggestion, or a different phrase or word. I believe the Spirit World was close by.

Many times I suggested that grieving persons pray to their loved one, for their loved one, and with their loved one. There truly is a Communion of Saints, and they, too, may have been or are now mystics!

REFLECTION

Take some deep and healing breaths. Move slowly through major times in your life and discover areas of pain—death or other pain. Have you accepted the reality of the loss? What were some of the behaviors or feelings you experienced? Physically? Emotionally? Mentally? Socially? Spiritually? Have you been aware of the four tasks of grief? Were they real for you? Is there more work to be done? Is there fear when you recognize that pain? Are you able to face it and transmute it into love, love of self?

SUGGESTION

Put on some relaxing music. Be present to your breathing. Let the music and your breathing calm you and allow that energy to be present as it lifts your spirit. There must be no judgment. This is extremely important.

This is not a time to judge the past or the present. It is a time for compassion—compassion for yourself! Now check into any pain that is present in your heart. As much as you can, pour love into that pain. Accept that God never left you alone in your pain. Release as many difficult feelings as possible at this time. Resolve to come back as often as needed to release a little more. Resolve to get help if needed.

WRITING OPTION

What? Do some free writing. Write the first thing that pops into your head as you say the following words:

- Grief
- Loss
- Death

- Change
- Identity
- Healing
- Love
- Saints or Angels
- God

Next, write a little about times when you have experienced the above.

So What? Write about why each of these experiences was so moving and powerful for you. Why do you think these particular experiences popped into your mind first when you worked through the list of words above?

What Now? Write about how you feel now after having experienced those events and how you plan to take some steps to help yourself heal and move on with your life. If your pain is particularly acute and de-bilitating, search the Internet, phonebook, or contact your place of worship to find numbers of grief counselors or a grief support group with whom you will speak about your pain.

After making an appointment to speak with someone or join a grief support group, jot down some questions you have and some goals you would like to achieve in working through your grief. Allow yourself to visualize what your life might be like after you have worked through your grief. What does it look like? What are you now able to do? Visualization is a powerful strategy that helps people move from thought to action.

EPILOGUE

And know that I am with you always,
until the end of the world.
(Matthew 28:20)

Mysticism
Consciousness
Enlightenment
Awareness

These words are often used inter-changeably. As we grow deeper in the spiritual life, we become more awake, more in touch with the reality of the Spirit World and the reality of the world around us. We have a desire to spend more time in prayer, meditation, and contemplation. We each do it in different ways according to our own personality and abilities. Yet, we must go on with our ordinary lives—whether it is washing dishes, cleaning the house, doing the job that we are grateful to have, or participating in the play and entertainment, which are so important for healthy lives.

There is a story about the Buddha that has been told many times. It is one that sets the stage for the emergence of humility and truth. The Buddha was asked by a disciple, "When will I know when I am Enlightened?"

The Buddha, in all his wisdom, calmly responded, "Before Enlightenment, you chop wood and carry water. After Enlightenment, you chop wood and carry water." This simple story serves to put life into perspective.

This same message comes out of the Christian tradition, as can be seen in many examples. One of my favorite stories is of Mary and Joseph. Both of them were privy to numerous experiences of dreams and visits from the higher realms, including direct and clear messages from angels. What gifts! They were surely "enlightened" beings! They were truly mystics! Yet, the knowledge and imagination that we have of their simple lives in Nazareth was that Mary washed dishes, cooked meals, mended the clothes of Joseph and Jesus, and did all the household work that was expected of a faithful Jewish housewife.

Joseph was the carpenter who fashioned tables and chairs and fulfilled the needs of his neighbors in Nazareth. Joseph must have been a wonderfully kind and gentle man. Therefore, it is my belief that he, being the loving person that he was, also made little gifts to surprise and favor the children of their little town. Even after having experienced the wonderful gifts that God had bestowed upon them, Joseph and Mary went about their ordinary, mundane tasks and responsibilities in life. In other words, after Enlightenment, they continued to "chop wood and carry water."

It is a wonderful thing to grow in the spiritual life, but the Christian's true identification is to recognize that just as Jesus was God's beloved, we are also. Just as Jesus is the Word, we are to be the word in our own time and space. Just as Jesus brought healing to His wounded world, we are called to bring healing to our own wounded world. Just as Jesus brought reconciliation to His world, we are called to bring reconciliation to ours. It is not enough to "follow Jesus" as we have been taught in our religion classes; we must be Him in our world today. This is the real identity of the Christian.

How do we go about answering this call? By meditating on the way Jesus lived His daily life as the Father's Word in His time. By spreading unconditional love for humankind and to find ways in our own times to do the same. Our work is to continue to recreate our lives, to be healers and reconcilers and persons caught up in the realization that "It is no longer I that live, but Christ lives in me" (Galatians 2:20). Only then have we identified with Jesus. Only in Communion with Him, will we find who we really are— one who is merging with the mind and heart of Christ! But we must ask.

Jesus was serious when He said, "Ask and you shall receive; seek and you shall find; knock and the door shall be opened to you. For whoever asks, receives; whoever seeks, finds; whoever knocks is admitted. What father among you will give his son a snake if he asks for a fish, or hand him a scorpion if he asks for an egg? If you, with all your sins, know how to give your children good things, how much more will the heavenly Father give the Holy Spirit to those who ask?" (Matthew 7:7-11)

When our whole being, together with the Spirit World and the Communion of Saints, pray together, the power of intention can change the world.

WRITING OPTION

I hope that in some way this book and the stories and exercises contained in it have helped you in some way to grow closer to Christ. If you would like to share some of your experiences, I would love to hear from you. So please write to me, and I will be happy to correspond with you as time allows. (My email address is provided in "About the Author" on page 223.)

ABOUT THE AUTHOR

Arlene Einwalter, MRE, MST, a School Sister of St. Francis, has been an educator, counselor, and spiritual mentor in the United States and in Australia. In all her ministry, Arlene has emphasized the importance of spirituality. While in Santa Fe, she founded Gerard's House, a center for grieving children from three to nineteen. Arlene is now retired and living in Milwaukee.

Arlene Einwalter can be reached via email at qarlene@gmail.com.

CPSIA information can be obtained
at www.ICGtesting.com
Printed in the USA
FFOW01n0819160714
6328FF